EXPLORERS WHO GOT LOST

By Diane Sansevere-Dreher

A TOM DOHERTY ASSOCIATES BOOK
NEW YORK

To Dylan Thomas Dreher

This is a work of fiction. All the characters and events portrayed in this book are either products of the author's imagination or are used fictitiously.

EXPLORERS WHO GOT LOST

Cover and interior art by Ed Renfro

A Tor Book
Published by Tom Doherty Associates, LLC
175 Fifth Avenue
New York, NY 10010

www.tor.com

Tor® is a registered trademark of Tom Doherty Associates, LLC.

ISBN: 0-812-52038-6

First edition: October 1992

Printed in the United States of America

0 9 8 7 6 5 4 3

CONTENTS

INTRODUCTION

During the fifteenth century just about every explorer who sailed beyond the horizon to find new lands thought he knew where he was going. But in fact most got terribly lost and stumbled on places no one had ever heard of before. That is why the 15th century began what is known as the "Age of Discovery."

Nowadays we merely look at a map to locate any particular spot on the planet. But to Europeans in the fifteenth century much of the world was a big mystery. Captains of sailing ships had only crude ideas of the geography of lands beyond their horizons. But curiosity was stirring among educated people, especially the kings and queens of countries that based much of their wealth on foreign trade. This period was unusual because for the first time, exploration was backed by the power and money of whole countries, not just adventurous individuals. Many explorers were sent out to find new trading routes, or they sailed off into the unknown to conquer distant lands and bring back treasure. Other explorers set out to convert the people they found to the Christian religion.

Whatever the reason, those explorers always had a destination in mind and a plan for getting there. But storms, accidents, lack of knowledge of the earth, plus crude navigational equipment, caused explorers to get lost. Some never found what they were looking for. Or else the lands they were seeking did not even exist. The lucky ones found lands that were previously unknown.

These are the stories of such explorers — the ones who got lost. Their discoveries may have been accidental, but they changed the map of the world and the course of history.

A LITTLE HISTORY

For centuries, sailors stood on Portugal's Cape Saint Vincent and looked out over the Atlantic Ocean in fear. To uneducated people, the place where the sea and sky met was the end of the earth. Many people believed that the world was flat and that anyone who ventured beyond the horizon would fall over the edge and land in Hell.

When Prince Henry of Portugal (who lived from 1394 to 1460) stood on that same spot, the horizon did not fill him with fear, but with wonder and a desire to know what lay beyond. He lived at just the right time and in just the right part of the world to be able to satisfy his desire. Portugal was the first European country to sponsor voyages into the unknown. Its location on the southwestern corner of Europe made it a good starting place. The Atlantic Ocean washed up on Portugal's shores and North Africa was not far away. But more important than that was the vision of Prince Henry himself. He is credited with beginning the Age of Discovery.

During the 14th century (1301 to 1400), the Portuguese began to build what later became an empire based on naval power. As a Christian country, Portugal was the natural enemy of the Moslem countries of North Africa. The Moslems, also known as Moors, made up what we know as the Arab world today. They had conquered large parts of Europe centuries earlier.

In the early 1400s the Portuguese finally succeeded in driving out the Moors. Then, in 1415, they took the war into northern Africa and captured the Moorish port of Cueta. Portugal now controlled the shipping lanes in and out of the Mediterranean Sea, which brought them closer to breaking the Moslems' tight grip on important trade routes.

Prince Henry was the third son of King John I of Portugal (who ruled from 1385 to 1433). As a young man in his twenties, the prince fought bravely in the battle for Cueta, an important seaport on the northwest coast of Africa. As a result, he was knighted by his father and made a duke. He returned to Cueta in 1418 to defend the stronghold when the Moors tried to recapture it.

In Cueta, the prince heard of the great centers of trade in Eastern Africa. There merchants traded pepper, cinnamon, nutmeg, cloves and other valuable spices that came from the Indies (China, Japan, India and the Spice Islands). They were highly prized by Europeans because food storage and cooking methods were very crude in those days and the spices were used to preserve and flavor meat.

In almost any business, a high demand for a product means a high price. Thus the spice trade was very profitable. The products were transported over a long overland route by Arab traders, who kept a tight hold on the business. At each stage on the journey to Europe, an Arab merchant would add a little to the price. By the time the spices reached their final destination, they were very expensive.

It is not hard to understand why European merchants were eager to find a shorter route to the source of the spices. A lot of money was at stake, so the kings and princes of Spain and Portugal would do almost anything to break the Arab monopoly.

Prince Henry also heard of a king named Prester John, who was thought to rule a rich Christian empire in Africa. However, historians have found that Prester John was only a myth. At the time, there were many myths and legends about faraway places and the people who lived there. Europeans believed the myths simply because they had no proof that they were not true.

When the prince returned from Cueta, he wanted to know all about Africa so he could trade with these new regions. He also wanted to find Prester John's kingdom and enlist the king's aid in fighting the Moslems. In addition, he began to wonder if there was a sea route to India. This would allow him to trade directly with the Indies and bypass the Arab traders. Prince Henry decided that the only way to find the answers to these questions was to send out explorers.

In 1416, to prepare for his voyages of exploration, the prince went to Cape Saint Vincent in Portugal. At a place called Sagres, he built a house and a chapel. Then he set up a vast library and brought navigators, ship captains, mapmakers, astronomers and geographers to Sagres to form Europe's first school of navigation. As a result of his dedication to exploration, he would become known to history as "Prince Henry the Navigator."

After studying the maps and the works of the specialists he had brought to Sagres, Henry believed that only Africa stood between Europe and India. But he did not know the size and shape of this continent, since no one had ever sailed beyond the grim red cliffs of Cape Bojador on the northwestern coast of Africa (near the Sahara Desert). Sailors did not attempt to go any farther south because they believed that the waters there boiled over sharp reefs where man-eating sea serpents lay in wait. If the boiling sea and the sea serpents did not kill them, the sailors were sure the burning, tropical sun would fry them to death.

These fears were not totally unjustified. In fact, at the foot of Cape Bojador there is a reef where the water churns and throws up clouds of spray, while haze and windblown sand from the desert darkens the sky. The sun cannot be seen and the sea actually becomes dark. When such awesome natural occurrences were combined with the general ignorance of the times, it is no wonder that the Atlantic Ocean became known as the "Sea of Darkness."

To make navigation less subject to guesswork, Prince Henry's scholars improved the astrolabe, the quadrant and the compass, which were the three primary navigational tools of the time. With better equipment, ships could now sail out of sight of land without getting lost, at least some of the time.

The prince also had his shipbuilders design a new type of sailing vessel, called the caravel. It was built in many shapes and sizes, but most were less than 100 feet long with a single deck and a small raised section at the stern called a *poop*. A caravel was faster and easier to maneuver than the clumsy carracks formerly used.

Prince Henry first sent his caravels out along the northern coast of Africa. He was too busy to go himself, but he ordered his captains to make maps and chart the currents, winds and water depths. He also ordered them to keep daily written records, known as logs. Until this time, few captains had ever kept such records.

Henry's ships sailed into the Atlantic Ocean and down the west coast of Africa. In 1420, an expedition found the Madeiras, a group of islands 350 miles off the northwest coast of Africa. In 1427, the prince's captains discovered the Azores, a group of islands 900 miles to the west of Portugal. But no one had yet tried to sail around Cape Bojador. Finally, in 1434, a Portuguese expedition led by a man named Gil Eanes rounded the cape and found, to their surprise, no boiling waters or sea serpents, but a calm bay.

Other captains sailed farther and farther south after that. They set up out-

posts to trade for gold. But Henry was not content with only gold. In 1441, he ordered his sailors to kidnap African natives to be sold in Europe as slaves. Although African tribes practiced slavery themselves, they were not ready for the large-scale raids of the Europeans. The slave trade quickly became very profitable for Portugal, and it provided the

SLAVERY — A PROFITABLE TRADE

Under the direction of Prince Henry the Navigator, Antao Goncalves brought the first African slaves back to Lisbon in 1441. Soon, Arab traders were raiding the interior of West Africa in order to supply the Portuguese demand. The Arabs kept their captives in stockades while awaiting the arrival of Portuguese caravels.

Although some captured Africans came from advanced cultures, Europeans thought all Africans to be primitive, heathen people who deserved to be enslaved by Christians.

Slave trading became a profitable business for Portuguese explorers. Between 1441 and 1500, fifty thousand African slaves were brought back to Portugal. In the 1600s, with the colonization of the Americas, the demand for slaves grew and the number of Africans sold into slavery increased until certain countries actually became dependent on slave labor.

main source of finance for the costly expeditions of discovery. The prince later tried to stop the trade, but the door to profits had been opened and it would not close for hundreds of years.

When Prince Henry the Navigator died in 1460, his captains had reached Cape Blanc, the Senegal River, Cape Verde and Sierra Leone to set up trading posts. The Portuguese markets were filled with gold dust, ivory, sugar cane, pepper and, of course, slaves. Portugal had become a major sea power and was eagerly seeking new sources of wealth, which meant more exploration.

By now, other countries, particularly Spain, were beginning to compete with Portugal for the riches that lay in undiscovered lands. Throughout Europe, young men, soldiers, ship captains, anyone with a thirst for adventure, sought employment in voyages of exploration. The Age of Discovery had begun.

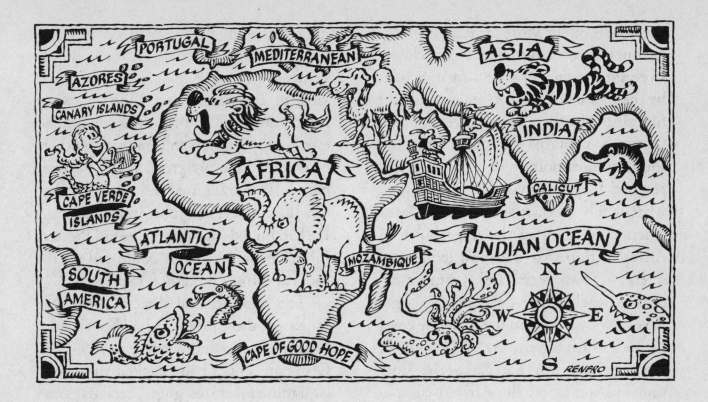

BARTOLOMEAU DIAS AND VASCO DA GAMA

After the death of Prince Henry in 1460, it seemed for a while that Portuguese exploration would end.

The prince's nephew now became King Alfonso V (who ruled from 1438 to 1481). He was more interested in driving the Moors out of Morocco than in exploration. However, he did give an exclusive five-year contract to a wealthy merchant by the name of Fernão Gomes, who sent his ships farther and farther south. Gomes's captains ventured past the southernmost point of Sierra Leone and reached Cape Palmas, off the coast of what is now known as the Ivory Coast. Then they rounded the huge bulge of Africa to find that the coast led almost due east. Two years later, Gomes's explorers reached the delta of the Niger River. Not far beyond the delta the coast turned south again. By 1474, one of Gomes's navigators had passed the equator. This point on the African coast is over 3,000 miles from Portugal and to Prince Henry's explorers there seemed to be no end to the continent.

Bartolomeau Dias was in Portugal during this exciting time. He had been born in 1450, and we know that he was a knight of the royal household. This meant that he had been knighted by King Alfonso, perhaps for a great feat of bravery in battle. Dias also must have been well-educated in horsemanship and weaponry. These skills were required in all the young men at court. When and where Dias acquired his training as a seaman is not known. But it is likely that he sailed on one or more voyages of discovery along the west coast of Africa.

In 1481, John, the great-nephew of Prince Henry the Navigator, became king of Portugal. King John II (who ruled from 1481 to 1495) was very interested in exploration and trade with other countries. Like his great uncle, he was particularly interested in reaching the kingdom of Prester John in east Africa. He had hoped that after he found Prester John, Portuguese ships could sail on to India and trade directly for spices.

The need to deal directly with the sources of these products had been made even more pressing because in 1453 the Ottoman Turks had blocked the overland route for spices, gold, precious gems and perfumes that came from China, Japan, India and the Spice Islands. The Turks were another group of Moslems who had been fighting with the Christians for centuries. European merchants now had to find a new way to obtain these goods. It seemed that the only way was by sea.

King John II had made a good start. Portuguese sailors had already explored large portions of Africa's coast. The king was determined to reach the southern end of the continent and sail around it to India. But no one knew how far the African coast extended.

In 1482, King John sent a man named

Diego Cão to find the end of the continent. Cão carried a number of *padrãos*, or stone pillars, bearing the date and the coat of arms of Portugal. He was to erect these monuments on prominent points along the coast to claim possession for Portugal. When he returned in 1484, a column stood on the shore of the Congo River and another on Cape Lobo, now called Cape Santa Maria. Cão thought he had just about reached the tip of Africa at that point.

King John was delighted and sent him back in 1485 to make the final turn into the Indian Ocean. This time Cão continued down the coast past what would become known as Cape Lobo, but discovered to his dismay that the coast seemed to run south forever. There was no end in sight. He erected his last *padrão* on the shore of Cape Cross in what is now Namibia. This was still 1,000 miles north of the southern tip of the continent.

King John was not discouraged that Cão had not reached the end of Africa. He was still determined to find it. Two years later, he sent Bartolomeau Dias to seek the route around Africa into the Indian Ocean.

Dias left Lisbon, Portugal, in August, 1487, with two caravels, the *São Cristóvão* and the *São Pantaleão*. The small fleet

THE CARAVELS

The design of the caravel produced speed and maneuverability. Unlike the big, round-bottomed carracks, which were made for holding large cargos, the caravel had a slimmer hull and a shallower keel. These features gave the caravel greater speed and allowed it to sail into shallow harbors and inlets. Another important feature was the fact that it was "lateen-rigged," with big triangular sails. The triangular sail could be set on either side of the mast to take advantage of the wind. Most caravels had two masts, each with its own lateen sail. Later caravels added a third mast that carried a square-rigged sail. This provided a wider surface of canvas to take advantage of stiff ocean winds. In contrast, carracks were "square-rigged," with rectangular sails set at right angles to the mast. These sails worked well when the wind blew from behind, but they were not good when the wind was blowing from the side, or when the ship had to sail into the wind.

also included a storeship filled with supplies. Dias knew from Cão that provisions were hard to find along the arid coast of southwest Africa. He hugged the coast and followed Cão's route along the African coastline past the Equator and Cape Lobo. Early in December, he moored the storeship in a sheltered bay in what is now southern Angola and continued south with his two caravels.

His ships passed desolate sand dunes that rose from the water's edge along the coastline. Dias named this area *Areias Gordas*, meaning "Broad Sands." He continued along the coast, sailing farther south than any Portuguese ship had ever dared.

In mid-January, 1488, according to 16th-century historians, the caravels were hit by a great storm. The raging seas tossed the tiny ships about. The fierce winds drove them south and they lost sight of land for almost two weeks. Sailing in the vast Sea of Darkness, the crews were frightened. No one had sailed that far from land before and they did not know what dangers lurked in the waters.

When Dias turned the caravels east to find land again, he found nothing but open water. He gradually figured out that he must have been blown past the end of the continent. So he changed course again and sailed north this time. But he had no idea where he was. Finally Dias sighted high mountains on the horizon. He assumed that they represented the southern tip of Africa. This meant that the coast ran not from north to south, but from east to west. Dias approached the land and anchored in what is now known as Mossel Bay, a place about halfway along the southern end of Africa.

On February 3, 1488, Dias stepped ashore. Awaiting him were many tall, black natives wrapped in animal skins. With them was a large herd of cattle. The natives were from a tribe of African herders who called themselves *Khoikhoi*, which means "men of men." They had never seen white men or huge ships before and thought that they must be from another world. Lacking weapons, the frightened natives threw stones at the Portuguese. In defense, the Portuguese killed one of the Khoikhoi. The natives quickly retreated with their cattle before Dias could learn anything about them or trade for fresh meat and water.

By now, the coast was stretching eastward, and Dias sailed on until he reached a bay that was later named Algoa Bay. Although he wanted to follow the coast farther, his crews were tired and

began to protest. Their provisions were low, their storeship was weeks behind, and the coastline seemed to go on forever. The sailors were afraid to proceed without knowing where the coast led and what they would find there.

Dias agreed to turn back, but asked for a few more days to sail along this new shore. The sailors agreed. The ships stopped at a place that would be named Cape Padrone and erected a *padrão*, or stone pillar, claiming this region for Portugal. After three more days of sailing, Dias could see that the coast led in a northeasterly direction. He had no doubt that he was now on the eastern coast of Africa and had reached the Indian Ocean. Somewhere across the water was India and the spices and treasures of the Far East. Dias wanted to continue sailing up the coast, but he had promised his crews that he would turn back. It must have been a painful moment because he actually knew where he was and could not take advantage of the fact.

Disappointed, Dias turned the little fleet about and headed back along the coast toward home. On the way, he spotted majestic mountains rising from the land. Near what is now called Table Mountain, he found a safe place to anchor and erected another stone pillar to claim the passage into the Indian Ocean

---

NAVIGATIONAL EQUIPMENT

The *astrolabe* was used to measure the angle of stars above the horizon. The *quadrant* measured the height of the sun and stars above the horizon. The two measurements determined a ship's latitude, which is its position north or south of the Equator. It is marked by imaginary horizontal lines that circle the earth at the same distance from the North and South Poles. Early explorers did not know how to plot longitude, which indicates a ship's position east or west of an imaginary line that circles the earth vertically through the North and South Poles.

The *compass* was used to set a course in any direction — north, south, east, or west.

---

for Portugal. The area would later become the city of Cape Town, the capitol of South Africa. Dias had found the southern tip of Africa, which he had missed on the outward voyage.

According to legend, Dias named this spot the Cape of Storms because of the fierce weather that drove him away from the land on his way to the Indian Ocean. However, when he returned to Portugal in December, 1488, the king changed the name to the Cape of Good Hope. This anticipated the opening of Portugal's sea route to India and the elimination of the Arab middlemen in the spice trade.

King John was so pleased that he

immediately made plans for a voyage around the Cape of Good Hope to find the route across the Indian Ocean to India. Unfortunately, the king died before his plans were completed.

The new king, Manuel I (who ruled from 1495 to 1521), carried on the exploration begun by the old king. He knew enough about India to realize that when his ships arrived there the captains would be dealing with civilized, rich Moslem merchants. Also, the traditional hostility between Moslems and Christians meant that the Portuguese would have to be very careful. The leader of the new expedition had to be a good ambassador and able to stand his ground in that civilized world. Obviously the king did not think Dias was the man for the job. His choice was a Portuguese navigator named Vasco da Gama.

Bartolomeau Dias's career was not over though. Vasco da Gama's fleet was to be the biggest and best organized of all expeditions the Portuguese had ever made. It was important that the ships be able to deal with anything they would meet. So the king asked Dias to design and equip four of the vessels. Under Dias's skillful supervision, the ships were outfitted with the most up-to-date navigational equipment and charts, plus batteries of cannon and numerous firearms.

On July 8, 1497, Bartolomeau watched as Vasco da Gama set out for the Cape of Good Hope and from there to India. Dias accompanied da Gama as far as the Cape Verde Islands (off the coast of today's Senegal) and then returned to Portugal. He knew that without his historic discovery of the southern tip of Africa, such an expedition to the Far East would not take place.

From the Cape Verde Islands, Vasco da Gama took an entirely new route to reach the southern tip of Africa. He headed away from the coast and boldly sailed out into the Atlantic Ocean. This southwest course was shorter and took advantage of the winds and currents. Although he did not know it, his course took him within 600 miles of Brazil and the South American continent, as yet undiscovered. This route is just about the same one used by ships today when sailing from Europe to the tip of Africa.

Five months after leaving Portugal, Vasco da Gama rounded the Cape of Good Hope. On December 16, his fleet sailed past the last stone pillar that Bartolomeau Dias had erected in 1488 on Cape Padrone. He then sailed up the east coast of Africa and reached what is now the country of Mozambique in February, 1498.

East African ports were a surprise to

the Portuguese. Instead of cowherds, they found shrewd merchants and Moslem ship captains who used the compass, the quadrant, and could read navigational charts. The people dressed in linen trimmed with silk and gold.

When the Sultan of Mozambique came aboard da Gama's ship, he was not impressed with the goods offered for trade. He wanted red cloth, but the Portuguese had none. He turned up his nose at the other trinkets the Portuguese had brought. At Mombasa, a city in what is now Kenya, the Europeans found a harbor filled with ships from other ports along the Indian Ocean.

As expected, the Portuguese were not welcomed. The Moslems disliked the Christians just as much as the Christians disliked Moslems. However, at Malindi, a port just north of Mombasa, da Gama was given a friendly welcome. The sultan there wanted the Portuguese to become his allies against his rival in Mombasa because they had the most powerful weapons in the Indian Ocean. At Malindi (also in Kenya), da Gama obtained a pilot to guide him on the final part of his journey across the Indian Ocean to India. The Portuguese made the trip in 23 days. After traveling 13,000 miles by sea, the fleet anchored in Calicut, India, now called Kozhikode.

Vasco da Gama proved to be an excellent ambassador for Portugal. Before he left, he persuaded Calicut's king to trade directly with Portugal. When da Gama returned to Portugal in July, 1499, he carried with him a message from the king, written on a palm leaf. It read:

> *"Vasco da Gama, a gentleman of your household, came to my country, whereat I was pleased. My country is rich in cinnamon, cloves, ginger, pepper and precious stones. That which I ask of you in exchange is gold, silver, corals and scarlet cloth."*

This letter opened up direct trade between Portugal and India, which meant vastly greater profits for Portuguese merchants and, of course, King Manuel I. That same year, the king

planned an even more ambitious voyage to India. He put together a fleet of 13 ships to carry back all the goods Portugal would acquire. The commander of the fleet would be Pedro Álvares Cabral, a member of the King's Council (which is probably why he was chosen). Although Cabral was a good diplomat, he had never sailed a ship before. For this voyage, highly experienced captains were needed, so Bartolomeau Dias was chosen to command four of the ships.

On March 19, 1500, the Portuguese fleet sailed for India. Cabral had planned to follow the same route that da Gama had taken. He and his captains hoped that winds would carry them around the Cape of Good Hope. But a storm forced the fleet off course.

On April 22, the crews were surprised to sight land off their starboard bow (the right side of the ship). Without instruments to measure how far west he had sailed, Cabral had gotten lost and reached what is now southeastern Brazil. This part of South America juts east into the Atlantic Ocean, pointing to the bulge of West Africa. But the distance between the two is about 1,900 miles. The Portuguese fleet had been blown more than 1,000 miles off course.

Cabral thought that they had reached an island and called it Land of the True Cross, claiming the discovery for Portugal. One ship had been lost at sea during the storm and another returned to Portugal with news of the "island." The other 11 ships stayed in Brazil for eight days and then headed out into the Atlantic toward the Cape of Good Hope.

On May 24, another violent storm hit the fleet. This time four ships sank. Unfortunately Bartolomeau Dias was on one of them. The other seven ships rounded the Cape of Good Hope, sailed up the eastern coast of Africa and across the Indian Ocean. They arrived in Calicut, India, on September 13. At Calicut, many crew members were killed in a battle with a band of Arab merchants. The fleet then sailed to Cochin and Cannanore, in India, where the ships were loaded with spices. They returned to Lisbon on June 23, 1501.

Bartolomeau Dias never did get to see the Cape of Good Hope again. The majestic cape he discovered marks the southern tip of Africa, and to this day it is the sight that seamen look for on their way to the Indian Ocean.

CHRISTOPHER COLUMBUS

In 1451 Christopher Columbus was born as Cristoforo Colombo in Genoa, Italy. The city sits right at the edge of the Mediterranean Sea on Italy's west coast. Historians do not know a lot about the explorer's younger years, but they think that Christopher did not go to school. He and his younger brothers, Bartholomeo and Diego, worked with their father, who wove cloth. But whenever he could, the boy sat on the docks to watch the ships come and go in the busy harbor and to listen to sailors talk of their adventures at sea.

As a youngster, Christopher took short sea voyages along the coast of Italy, selling his father's wool cloth. Every change in the wind, every turn in the current and every harbor was a new and exciting adventure to the young sailor.

He did not know anything about navigation and got lost a few times, but he always managed to find his way by following the coastline.

At 15, Christopher left home to work on trading ships sailing back and forth on the Mediterranean Sea. During these voyages, he improved his sailing skills. He learned how to navigate by studying the height of the North Star at night and the position of the sun at noon. He learned how to use a compass. He could also tell where he was by watching birds, fish, driftwood, seaweed and the color of the water. The sea had much to teach him, and by learning its lessons well he hoped to someday discover many of the world's secrets.

At this time in history, many educated people in Europe knew that the world was round. Since the time of the ancient Greeks, mathematicians and geographers had known that they lived on a sphere, but they could not agree on how big it was. They were familiar with large stretches of the "Ocean Sea," which is what they called the Atlantic Ocean, but they did not know how wide it was. They knew that Africa and Asia existed, but could say very little about their geography and climate.

Europeans also knew about a place far to the east that they called the "Indies,"

meaning most of eastern Asia — China, Japan, India and the Spice Islands. Gold, spices, jewels and perfumes from these lands entered Europe by passing through merchant after merchant over a complicated land route. The route stretched thousands of miles across Central Asia to the great city of Constantinople. From there the goods were sent to Europe by ship, wagon and pack train. As a Christian city in North Africa, Constantinople had been a thorn in the side of the Turkish Empire for centuries. Finally, in 1453, the Turks captured the city and closed the trading route. Now European merchants had to figure out another way to get to the Indies — by sea.

Whoever discovered a new route would become rich. The leaders of Portugal were determined to be the first ones to find that route. From all over Europe, map makers, navigators, astronomers and merchants came to Portugal to take part in the great quest. Portuguese vessels sailed along the west coast of Africa, trying to find a way around the continent to the Indies. Storms, shipwrecks, pirates and disease claimed many ships and sailors. But the lure of fame and riches provided a steady stream of willing adventurers to continue the search.

Portugal was certainly a place for someone like Christopher Columbus to be. However, it was only by accident that he wound up there.

In 1476, at the age of 25, Christopher sailed with a fleet of ships from Genoa carrying valuable cargo to England. When the ships neared Portugal, they were suddenly attacked by pirates. Cannonballs flew back and forth as the two fleets battled furiously throughout the day. Christopher was wounded and then flung into the sea when his ship exploded and sank. All of his shipmates were killed, but he was lucky. Spotting a floating oar, he grabbed it and kicked his way six miles through the sea to shore. Bleeding and tired, he dragged himself up on land. Christopher was convinced that God had saved him so that he could perform great works.

After he recovered from the shipwreck, Christopher went to Lisbon, Portugal, where his brother Bartholomeo was living. At the time, Lisbon was the busiest seaport in Europe. The city faced the ocean and its harbor was teeming with ships that traded with ports on the African coast. It was just the place for a young man seeking a life of exploration. Columbus got a job at the chart-making shop where his brother worked and quickly learned the skills of mapmaking. Soon the two brothers set up their own business. For eight years, Christopher

stayed in Lisbon, running the map shop, talking to sailors about their trips and making maps of the places they had been. He also made a number of long voyages himself.

Portuguese seamen had already explored sections of the African coast. They had ventured into the Ocean Sea and discovered a group of islands west of Portugal called the Azores. They had also set up colonies in the Madeiras, a group of islands off the west coast of Africa. They were sailing farther and farther north to find new lands and trade routes. Gradually the known world was becoming bigger and bigger.

During Columbus's chart-making and voyaging days, he began to have ideas of his own about how to get to the Indies. He had read a book written by Marco

Polo, who had traveled to the Indies two hundred years before by the overland route. Marco Polo wrote of the riches of the Great Khan in Cathay (China) and the island of Cipangu (Japan) with its golden rooftops. Christopher decided that he was going to beat everyone in the race to the Indies.

He thought the king of Portugal was going about it the wrong way. The king was sending ships down the west coast of Africa to find a way around the continent to the east. Christopher, however, thought there was a shortcut — to sail west to the Indies — straight across the Ocean Sea (the Atlantic Ocean).

There was a reason why no one had yet tried to sail across the Ocean Sea. It was known as the "Sea of Darkness." Most sailors believed that its waters ran dark, cold and rough. They thought it was so big that it would take years to cross. Certainly they would run out of food and water before ever reaching land again. And there was no way to get back. They knew that the world was round, and to their way of thinking, the trip west was downhill. This meant that the trip back would be uphill! Clearly the scientific thinking of the time was not very advanced. Thus many people thought Christopher had a crazy idea.

But Christopher read more and more books. He found some that agreed with his idea. The books that did not agree, he stopped reading. Finally he arrived at an estimate of the size of the globe. From this he figured that Japan was 2,400 miles due west from the Canary Islands, which lay about 60 miles off the northwest coast of Africa. China should be another 1,500 miles farther on, he reasoned. Columbus also managed to get his hands on a map made by Paolo Toscanelli dal Pozzo, a famous Italian astronomer and mathematician. This showed Japan and China sitting right where he thought. Now he had proof that the trip was not far at all.

But it was not only books that convinced Columbus that he was right. He believed that God had revealed the secrets of the world to him and had chosen him to be the first to find the sea route to the Indies. As far as Christopher was concerned, nothing that had happened to him had been an accident. God had planned everything: his birthplace, his shipwreck, finding his brother in Lisbon and even the choice of his name. In Latin, Christopher means "Christ-bearing," and young Columbus remembered the story of Saint Christopher, who is supposed to have carried the Christ Child across the dark waters of a river. He believed that he was meant to take the Christian religion across the Ocean Sea and convert the people in the Indies.

Columbus was sure that God had even arranged his marriage. Two years after he arrived in Portugal, he married a woman named Dona Felipa. They had a son whom they named Diego. Dona Felipa came from a noble family with friends in high places. This meant that Christopher was no longer just a common seaman, but a person with family influence.

Now all he needed was money, men and ships for his voyage. In 1484, Columbus went to King John II of Portugal (the son of Alfonso V, who ruled when Prince Henry the Navigator was alive). He showed him charts, mathematical calculations and even quotes from the Bible about the size of the ocean. He told the king about things he had seen during his voyages, such as exotic fruits washed up on the shores near Spain, and bodies of strange-looking people found in the sea. Columbus was so sure of his plan that he bragged to the king that he would make Portugal rich.

Unfortunately King John and his advisers thought that Christopher Columbus was just a big talker. The king said no to his plan of sailing west across the Ocean Sea in order to get to the Indies. The king would keep sending out ships to sail east around the tip of Africa. It was

a long route, but at least the Portuguese sailors knew where they were going.

Christopher was more determined than ever to find someone to back his voyage. His wife had died that same year and he now had no more reason to stay in Portugal. So he packed his belongings and with his five-year-old son, Diego, he left for Spain. When they arrived in the sleepy port of Palos, Columbus noticed a Franciscan monastery known as La Rábida. This turned out to be the solution to his problem of what to do with his son. The monks liked Columbus and offered to raise and educate Diego.

Columbus was very hopeful that King Ferdinand V and Queen Isabella I of Spain (who ruled jointly from 1474 to 1504) would say yes to his plan. The queen, after all, was a devout Christian. She insisted that everyone in Spain be a Christian, too. Columbus felt sure the queen would understand that crossing the Ocean Sea to the Indies was not only a way to make Spain rich, but a way to convert more people to Christianity.

Columbus went to a city named Cordoba, where the king and queen were living at the time. But there was one problem. The queen was too busy to see Columbus. It took him nine months to arrange a meeting, and when he did explain his plan, she didn't say yes. But she

didn't say no either. The queen was close to Christopher in age and liked him. She was impressed by his enthusiasm and she particularly liked his idea of spreading Christianity. The queen said he must wait until Spain won its war against the Moors who were holding Granada, a territory in southern Spain. The royal treasury was spending all of its money on winning the war.

Columbus settled down in Cordoba and waited. Weeks, months went by and still he waited. In the meantime, he fell in love with a woman named Beatrice Enriquez de Harana and soon he was the father of a second son, named Fernando. Although he loved Beatrice, he did not marry her because she was the daughter of a peasant. He felt that such a marriage was unsuitable for a man of his standing.

He had forgotten that he was the son of a simple weaver.

After three years of waiting for the queen to make up her mind, Columbus became angry and decided to go back to Portugal to try to talk to King John again. The explorer Bartolomeau Dias had just returned from sailing around the southern tip of Africa, opening up the sea route to the Indies for Portugal. But once again, King John was not interested in Christopher Columbus's silly ideas about crossing the Ocean Sea.

Columbus returned to Spain. He waited three more years. These were the worst years of his life. He just sat and waited for the queen to finish her war with the Moors. Finally, around Christmas, 1491, Queen Isabella called him to the royal court. She was ready to help him.

Christopher was very excited. But he was still very angry about the years he had spent waiting. He decided that Spain would now have to pay him well for his services. He told King Ferdinand and Queen Isabella that he wanted to be made a nobleman and be called "Admiral of the Ocean Sea." He wanted to be made viceroy and governor-general of all the lands he might discover. Furthermore, he wanted ten percent of all the riches — gold, silver, gems, spices and anything else of value he brought back to Spain. In addition, all his privileges were to be passed on to his heirs.

The king and queen could hardly believe their ears. The king flatly refused him. Queen Isabella tried to get Columbus to change his mind, but he would not listen. He lost his temper and left the royal court in a rage. Columbus was determined to make the voyage his way or not at all. He got on his mule and set out to see the king of France.

But Queen Isabella changed her mind. After all, if he did not succeed, he would get nothing. If, however, he did succeed, ten percent and a few titles was a small price to pay. She sent a messenger after him. Christopher Columbus had finally won. On April 17, 1492, the contract was signed, giving Columbus everything he asked for.

Palos, where Columbus had arrived six years earlier, was to be the port of departure. Three ships were chosen: the *Niña*, the *Pinta* and the *Santa María*. The *Niña* was the smallest, about 65 feet long; the *Pinta* was the fastest; the *Santa María* was the largest (and the slowest) — over 80 feet long. Columbus decided to command the *Santa María*.

Next he needed crews for his ships. But no one volunteered. Columbus was a foreigner and many thought he was a crazy one at that. Common sailors at that time still harbored many superstitions about the Sea of Darkness, or the Atlantic Ocean. They believed there were sea serpents so big that they swallowed ships whole, whirlpools that sucked ships down to the bottom of the sea and many other horrors that lurked in the unknown.

Finally, Martin Pinzón, one of the finest navigators in Spain, volunteered for the voyage. However, Columbus did not fully trust Pinzón and thought he would not follow orders. But he knew he needed him to find crews for his ships. Men had sailed with him before and respected him. If Martin Pinzón was going, they would go too. Soon, Pinzón had 90 men signed up for the voyage. He would command the *Pinta*, and his brother, Vicente, would command the *Niña*. Columbus also took along a man who spoke Arabic. (Arabic was such a foreign-sounding language that he thought the people of the Indies must speak it.)

With ships and men ready, Columbus now needed supplies. Each ship needed firewood, compasses, time-keeping devices, spare sails and spars, water, wine, sea biscuits, salt meats, cheese, beans, rice, almonds and sardines. The list was endless. Columbus took along

THE SPANISH INQUISITION

King Ferdinand and Queen Isabella believed that everyone in Spain had to practice Christianity. To this end, they set up what is known as the Spanish Inquisition. This arm of the Catholic Church looked for people who were supposedly not faithful to the teachings of the Catholic Church. They were called "heretics." Anyone thought to be a heretic was put on trial. If found guilty, a person was usually sentenced to cruel punishment. During the Inquisition, thousands of Jews and Moors were expelled from the country and thousands more were burned at the stake. As a result, Spain lost many of its most productive citizens and was never the same afterward.

cannons, muskets and crossbows in case the natives were not friendly. If they turned out to be friendly, he had small hawk bells, scissors, knives, coins, glass beads, needles and mirrors to trade for gold and other treasures he might find. He also brought cats to kill the rats that were always on board ships.

The king and queen gave Columbus three letters to take with him to the Indies. One was for Kublai Khan (a Chinese ruler who had been dead for nearly 200 years). The other two had spaces for the names of rulers to be filled in.

After three months of preparation, on the night of August 2, 1492, Columbus led his men to La Rábida's church to pray for a safe voyage. Many of the sailors were nervous about the trip, but they vowed to obey the admiral's commands.

As the sun was rising on the morning of August 3, 1492, Christopher Columbus, the Admiral of the Ocean Sea, stood on the poop of the *Santa María* and shouted, "Hoist anchor!"

Columbus was a happy man when sailing over the rolling sea with the wind at his back. In the first hour he began to write the log (record) of the voyage. He decided he would put down every detail: the direction and strength of the winds, types of birds, the fish they caught, currents, cloud patterns, and distances traveled each day with various sail combinations.

But the sailors were not as content as Columbus. They thought that leaving on a Friday was already a sign of bad luck. Then on the third day out at sea, the *Pinta*'s rudder broke — more bad luck. The ships stopped at the Canary Islands, Spain's territory off the coast of Africa, to repair the *Pinta* and take on more supplies. Then on September 6th, they pulled up anchor and sailed into the unknown.

"West!" Columbus shouted. The trade winds filled the sails and the ships moved quickly over the calm sea. After three days, land disappeared from sight.

As the wind blew, the three ships sailed farther and farther into uncharted seas, and the crews became more frightened. Who knew what could happen to them in the unknown? Day after day, the fleet sailed west. Columbus used maps and compasses and studied the stars, but he was forced to guess a lot about distance and direction. He estimated that they sailed about 140 nautical miles a day. (A regular mile measures 5,280 feet and a nautical mile is about 800 feet longer.)

After three weeks on the open sea, the ships ran into a giant bed of seaweed that stretched as far as the men could see. The air stilled and the sails went limp. The ships had entered an area of the North Atlantic called the Sargasso Sea. An eerie quiet filled the air, when suddenly a meteor streaked across the sky and disappeared into the sea.

Prepared to be scared by any unusual event, the sailors let their fears overtake them. They thought that the heavens were beginning to plunge into the sea and that they would never escape from the sea of weeds.

But the wind soon rippled the sails and the ships began to move slowly through the weeds. Then the wind picked up and drove them farther west. The men now feared they would never

be able to return home against such winds, particularly *uphill*.

Columbus thought that his sailors were fools. But he had ways to quiet their fears. For one thing, he kept two logs — one with the actual distances traveled and another that showed shorter distances. This one he showed the crew so they would not know how far they had really travelled from land. He also pointed out birds and marine life as signs that land was near.

With the promise of a reward for the first man to sight land, the sailors began to keep a close watch. Columbus, by his reckoning, thought that they should have reached the Indies by now.

At sunset on September 25, 1492, Martin Pinzón, captain of the *Pinta*, yelled out, "Land! Land!" The sailors danced and prayed on the deck that night. Columbus fell to his knees and thanked God. But by morning there was no sign of land anywhere. Pinzón had seen only a line of clouds close to the horizon.

On October 7, the *Niña* fired a cannon, which meant that land had finally been sighted. But again there was no land. Every day the men cried, "Land!" and every day it turned out to be a false alarm. In a rage, Columbus told his sailors that any man responsible for another false sighting would not be able to claim the reward if he did finally sight land.

The crews of the three little ships were sure that they were lost in the unknown forever. Finally they panicked. On the *Santa María* the men shouted and raced for the quarterdeck to take over the ship. Columbus held them back with a gun. He asked the sailors to give him three more days because he was sure that they were right off the coast of Cipangu (Japan). The crew backed off and agreed to give him three more days. "West!" he commanded.

The next day there were more signs of land. The sailors found a carved stick floating in the water and a branch with buds and flowers. They also saw a flock of birds fly southwest overhead. For the first time, Columbus changed his course. He decided to follow the birds. "Southwest!" he commanded. Now he was really sure that land would be sighted soon, so he promised a fine silk coat to the first person to do so.

That night at ten o'clock, Columbus spotted a light near the horizon that looked like a flickering candle. But the light disappeared. At two o'clock in the morning, the *Pinta* fired a cannon. A sailor named Rodrigo shouted, "Land Ho! Land Ho!" There was no doubt this time. In the moonlight, the crews of the three ships could see white cliffs. On October 12, 1492, Columbus had at last found Japan, or so he thought.

At dawn, the ships were in full view of a sandy white beach lined with palm trees. Beyond stood a jungle of green trees and bushes, dotted with bright flowers and strangely colored birds. Columbus was sure that he had reached the Indies, fulfilling the plan that God had for him. That day he proudly carried the royal flag of Spain up to the beach. He placed the flagpole in the sand and claimed the land for Spain. He then set a large cross in the ground and named his discovery San Salvador, which in Spanish means "Holy Savior." The island is part of what is called the Bahamas chain today.

Columbus became quite puzzled, however, when he saw naked people of a copper-brown color hiding among the trees. They looked nothing like the rich Orientals he expected to find in Japan. The natives gathered by the hundreds behind the trees. Curiosity finally overcame their fears and they edged from cover and timidly approached, armed with bone-tipped spears. Columbus saw that their bodies were painted red, black and other colors and that a few older men wore gold rings in their noses.

Columbus encouraged them to come

closer by gesturing in a friendly way. Since he thought that he had reached the Indies, he called the natives "Indians."

While the Spaniards thought the inhabitants of San Salvador were strange, it is hard to imagine how weird Columbus and his men appeared to the natives. They had never seen white men before and thought perhaps they were gods or birds from the sky. The natives touched the Spaniards' beards and hands and seemed amazed that they covered their bodies. They felt Columbus's clothing and ran their hands along the edges of his sword.

Columbus gave the natives little bells and placed necklaces of glass beads around their necks. The natives invited the sailors to stay and brought them exotic fruits and cassava bread to eat. They also gave them tamed parrots, spears and balls of cotton thread. But it was the gold

NATIVE AMERICANS

Thinking that he had reached the Indies, Columbus called the inhabitants of North America "Indians." Today we use the term "Native Americans." But in order to show events through the eyes of the explorers, the term "Indian" has been used throughout most of the text.

AMERICA — THE NEW WORLD

On October 12, 1492, when Christopher Columbus first sighted the island he called San Salvador (now known as Watlings Island in the Bahamas), he thought he had reached islands off the coast of Asia. In 1497, Amerigo Vespucci, an Italian navigator who made voyages for both Spain and Portugal, claimed that the land was not Asia, but a vast continent of a "new world."

In 1507, a German mapmaker, in the mistaken belief that Amerigo Vespucci was the first European to reach the southern part of the New World, credited him as the discoverer. Thus the name Amerigo was given to both the northern and southern continents, eventually becoming "America."

nose rings that interested Columbus and his men.

The Spaniards' interpreter was of no use in communicating with the Indians, so Columbus used sign language instead. He pointed to the gold nose rings and made gestures in an attempt to find out where the gold had come from. The natives pointed and gestured too, but they only copied whatever the Spaniards did. Finally they seemed to understand his question and pointed to the south and to the west.

Although these natives were poor and not what he expected to find in Cipangu, Columbus was still sure that he had found the Indies. But perhaps he was a little lost. He figured that San Salvador must be an island off the coast of Cipangu (that is, Japan). Actually, it is part of the chain below the southern tip of Florida known as the Bahamas.

Two days later, eager to find gold, Columbus set sail again. He took six Indians with him as guides. For two weeks the three ships sailed from island to island. But they were all very much like the first. The natives were friendly, but poor. And the few gold ornaments they found always came from some other place.

The Indians on board spoke of a place called Colba. Columbus thought Colba must be Cipangu, but that the natives were not pronouncing the word correctly. Actually the place they spoke of was what we know as Cuba. When Columbus arrived at this large island on October 28, he could see that it was not Japan. He recalculated his position and decided it must be the mainland — China. When he pointed to the interior of this new land, the natives cried, "Cubanacan!" He decided that this was the Indian name for Kublai Khan of China.

Columbus sent the interpreter and a few hand-picked men with the letter of introduction from the king and queen.

But there was no royal city. The only thing the men found was a village of 50 thatched-roof huts.

If Columbus was disappointed, he did not record it in the log he kept. He sailed for weeks among the small islands off the north coast of Cuba, recording all the marvelous things he saw — multicolored fish, beautiful birds, flowers and sweet fruits. There were many strange things he saw as well — dogs that didn't bark, hanging beds (hammocks), mermaids (really manatees), human skulls and bones left by cannibals, canoes that held forty men, and a dried leaf that men rolled up, lighted at one end and smoked (a cigar). But there was never any gold!

Martin Pinzón soon tired of this fruitless journey and set out on his own in the *Pinta* to find gold. Columbus had always been suspicious of Pinzón, and when he deserted the fleet, the admiral was not surprised. But he was very angry and he decided to sail on without him.

On December 6, the *Santa María* and the *Niña* landed in what is now Haiti. The crews were immediately attacked by swarms of mosquitos. There were so many that Columbus named the area the "Bay of Mosquitos." Despite the insects, it was a beautiful green island with many trees and mountains. Columbus and his men were reminded of Spain. The native women looked Spanish, the fish tasted like Spanish fish, even the trees were similar to trees found in Spain. He named the island *Hispaniola,* meaning "Little Spain." It is located 600 miles southeast of Florida. Today the Republic of Haiti occupies the western third and the Dominican Republic the eastern two thirds.

The natives were the friendliest Columbus had met in all his travels. Many visited the ships and were given bells and other trinkets. One day a nearby king by the name of Guacanagari sent Columbus a gift of hammered gold. The admiral asked where the gold came from. The natives told him that the source was a place called Cibao in the central part of the island. Columbus again thought they meant Cipangu.

Once again he set sail for Japan. The admiral and his crew had been so busy mingling with the natives that they had not slept in two days. On the evening of December 24, while sailing along the northern coast of Hispaniola, Columbus went to bed and left the helmsman in charge. But the helmsman was sleepy too, and he left the ship's boy in charge. Suddenly, around midnight, the ship ran aground on a coral reef. Columbus rushed to the deck and gave orders to try to save the ship. The *Santa María* began

SLAVERY

In the first settlement of the New World at Hispaniola, the Spanish forced many Indians into slavery. The Indians, however, did not make very good slaves.

In 1505, the Spanish began to import Negro slaves from Portugal. As other islands in the Caribbean were conquered, the demand for slaves to do the work grew rapidly. The supply from Portugal, however, was limited. By 1518, the Portuguese were shipping blacks from the west coast of Africa directly to the settlers in the New World.

As the slave trade grew more and more profitable, control passed from the Portuguese to the Spanish, to the Dutch, and finally to the English. Black men, women and children were crammed into ships for the crossing of the Atlantic Ocean. The conditions were so terrible that almost half died before reaching the New World. The trade ended in the 19th century, but by then, about ten million blacks had been sold into slavery in the Americas.

to leak and tilt on its side.

Columbus wept when he saw his ship begin to sink. He sent to the friendly king for help in unloading all the cargo. The king organized hundreds of the natives to unload the sinking ship until everything on board was removed. When they had finished, nothing had been lost or stolen.

King Guacanagari tried to comfort Columbus. He placed a plate of gold around his neck, knowing how much Columbus liked gold. In return, the admiral gave the king a shirt and a pair of gloves. Then he fired a musket. The king was spellbound when he saw the power of the weapon. He gave Columbus a mask with gold eyes and ears and other jewels. This time Columbus gave the king a scarlet coat, a silver ring and colored boots.

With all the gold the king had given him, Columbus began to think that there was a mine somewhere on the island. To him the loss of the *Santa María* was a sign from God that he would find gold in Hispaniola.

Columbus decided to sail back to Spain, leaving 40 men on the island to find the mine and dig for gold. He stocked the fort with goods and weapons and ordered the men to collect gold until he returned with more ships to pick them up. He also told the sailors to treat the natives kindly. Columbus named the new fort La Navidad.

On January 4, 1493, the *Niña* started for home. Two days later, the *Pinta* reappeared and joined Columbus for the voyage back to Spain. Martin Pinzón had many excuses for departing from the fleet. Columbus listened, but he did not believe him.

For the first few weeks the crews were delighted to see how well they sailed *uphill.* Then after six weeks the sea began to swell and the sky grew stormy. It was a hurricane. The waves crashed over the ships and the *Pinta* was blown out of sight of the *Niña*. Columbus flashed lamps to the *Pinta*, which answered faintly. When the signal stopped, Columbus thought that the other ship had sunk. The *Pinta*, however, had not sunk. It was on its way back to Spain. Pinzón was hoping to beat Columbus and claim all the glory. But by the time he reached Spain, Pinzón had become quite sick. He dragged himself home and died without seeing the king and queen.

On March 15, seven and a half months after they had left, Columbus and his crew arrived back in Spain. The news spread quickly that Columbus had found the Indies. Soon the Admiral of the Ocean Sea was being treated as a great hero. All across Spain, people poured out to see Columbus and his strange procession making its way to Barcelona to see the king and queen.

The admiral led the parade, richly dressed and ornamented in gold. He was followed by the six Indians wearing aprons, gold nose rings, beads and bracelets. Then came men carrying treasures from the Indies: cages of parrots, baskets of plants, shells, thread and, most important, samples of gold.

Columbus's big moment of triumph came when he reached the royal court. Inside the great hall, King Ferdinand and Queen Isabella stood to greet their admiral. They invited him to sit beside them while he told the story of his voyage and discoveries.

Columbus gave them colored parrots and belts made of fish bone. He showed them trays of gold objects and presented the six painted Indians. Queen Isabella was full of compliments. She thought that what Columbus had done was a miracle. Columbus was treated like royalty and for the next six weeks, he remained at court, basking in glory. He was so proud that he even began to sign his name in a new way:

.S.
.S.A.A.
S M X
:Xpo FERENS./

No one knows exactly what this means, but the strange signature combines Greek and Latin initials and might mean, "Christopher [Christ-bearing] servant of the Most High Savior."

News about the discoveries travelled fast. Everyone believed that Columbus had found the Indies. The king and queen wanted him to go back and settle more land and bring back gold and spices for Spain. For the return voyage Columbus had no difficulty finding sailors. He told them that they could look for gold, but they must also work on the land and plant crops.

On September 25, 1493, Columbus set sail again. This time he had 17 ships and 1,500 men. He took five personal servants and six priests to convert the natives. The ships carried horses, sheep, cows, goats, pigs and chickens. The cargos included seeds and grapevines to plant, plus tools, weapons and enough wine to last two years.

It was an easy voyage. Columbus steered a more southerly route and the trip took less than a month. He landed first at an island, which he named *Domenica*, "Day of Discovery." But he quickly left when he found that it was inhabited by people he thought were cannibals. Spurred by the vision of a fort filled with gold, Columbus sailed on, arriving at Hispaniola on the evening of November 27.

The admiral expected a grand reunion with the 40 men left behind at La Navidad. But there was no sign of life at the fort. Columbus fired cannons, but there was no answer. The next morning Columbus and his men went ashore. He could not believe his eyes. The fort had been burned to the ground and there were no Spaniards in sight.

Columbus visited Guacanagari, the native king who had helped him in the past. The king told him that some of the settlers had been killed when they fought over Indian women and gold. The rest, he said, were killed by a native tribe angry with the settlers for kidnapping their women and stealing their gold. Guacanagari said he had tried to help the Spaniards, but there had been too many of the fierce natives.

Columbus immediately decided to abandon La Navidad as an unlucky place. In May, 1494, he chose a new site on Hispaniola and named it Isabela, after the queen of Spain.

But his second attempt to set up a colony failed miserably. The place he chose was far from fresh water and infested with mosquitos, which carry malaria, a disease that causes high fever and chills. The warm, humid climate and native food made the men sick, too. Their own food supply ran low and the sailors did not want to spend the time planting crops. Worst of all, there was no gold.

Columbus decided to send some ships back to Spain for more supplies to keep the settlement going. But how could he do this without sending gold? Although he managed to scrape up some gold, it did not amount to much. So he loaded 12 of his ships with cinnamon, pepper and sandalwood, hoping that would be sufficient to impress the king and queen.

While the ships sailed for Spain, Columbus led an expedition inland to search for the gold mine he believed was there. His men did find some gold in rocks and sand along the riverbank, but there was no gold mine. Columbus decided to leave his brother Diego in charge of Isabela and go to what he thought was mainland China (really Cuba).

Columbus was convinced that he had found the Indies. But to be sure that no one disagreed with him, he made his sailors sign a paper, swearing that they had found the land of silk and spices. Columbus sailed for five months around the islands, but he did not find much gold and discovered only one significant island, which is known as Jamaica today. So he returned to Isabela.

By this time, Columbus was suffering from gout, which was very painful and caused him to sleep a lot. He was happy to find that his brother Bartholomeo had arrived from Spain with three more ships. Columbus needed this good news because he heard a lot of bad news upon his return. The mosquitos were thicker than ever. Disease had swept throughout the settlement and food was in short supply. The men were stealing from the natives and starting fights. Hoping to control the situation, Columbus appointed Bartholomeo as governor of Isabela. But this made some of the settlers angry. They stole three ships and sailed back to Spain to tell the king and queen what a poor job Columbus was doing and that he had lied about finding gold.

For the next year and a half, Columbus and his brothers tried to salvage Isabela. But the Indians were tired of being treated like slaves. They resisted and violence broke out. Columbus decided to punish them. Although there were thousands of natives, the Spaniards had horses and crossbows. It was no contest. The natives were defeated and many were slaughtered.

During the fighting, Columbus's men captured hundreds of Indians. In despair over not finding gold, he sent 500 of them to Spain to be sold as slaves. Since converting the Indians had gone as badly as the gold mining, most were not Christians. Thus the Spaniards felt that it was not wrong to enslave them.

Columbus now introduced a new system to bring in gold. He ordered every male over 14 to fill a small bell with gold

dust every three months. But no matter how hard they worked, the natives could not find enough. They were cruelly punished. Many ran off to the hills and hid and others fled the island. Between 1494 and 1496, one third of the natives of Hispaniola were killed, enslaved, or scared away by the Spanish explorers.

In March, 1496, Columbus decided to return to Spain to answer charges that he was mishandling the natives. He knew he had much explaining to do to the king and queen. When he arrived in Spain this time, there was no cheering. In fact, many people had heard about his troubles in the Indies and called him "Admiral of the Mosquitos"!

It never occurred to Columbus that he might have calculated wrong and gotten lost. He thought that he did not find gold because God was punishing him for being too proud. Deciding to humble himself, Columbus put on the plain brown robe of a monk and wore a scratchy shirt next to his skin to prove that he was God's servant.

Wearing the robe, Columbus went to see the king and queen. As before, he brought parrots, natives, a little gold and tropical curiosities. But no one was impressed. The queen, however, was not quite ready to give up on Columbus. She wanted him to go back and to work harder at converting the natives to Christianity.

It took Columbus more than a year to prepare for the third voyage. No one volunteered for the trip, so men were taken out of the prisons to send on the voyage. On May 30, 1498, the Admiral of the Ocean Sea set sail with eight ships. Five sailed to Hispaniola with supplies. Columbus led the other three on a voyage farther south than he had been before. The first island he came upon he named *Trinidad* because he had dedicated his third voyage to the Holy Trinity (the Christian concept of three persons in one God — the Father, the Son and the Holy Spirit).

From Trinidad he sailed west to South America. Columbus thought it was just another island, not a whole continent. He wasn't expecting to find one and it didn't fit into the picture of geography he had in his head.

Columbus spent two weeks exploring the coast of Venezuela (located at the top of South America). He found fresh-water rivers, which made him think that he had found more than just another island. It must be a part of Asia, he thought. Columbus still did not understand that he had discovered a whole new world.

Bad health forced the admiral to sail on to Santo Domingo (on the southern coast of Hispaniola and today the capitol of the Dominican Republic). When he arrived, he found problems awaiting him. Bartholomeo had tried to move the settlement to Santo Domingo. But the settlers had run into trouble with the Indians and fighting had broken out.

Food was scarce and this caused discontent to spread among the Spaniards. They were becoming ungovernable because their expectations of getting rich had crumbled. A group of rebels led by a man named Roldan tried to take over the island. Finally, several hundred returned to Spain and complained bitterly about Columbus.

King Ferdinand and Queen Isabella decided to send an inspector to Hispaniola to find out what was going on. On August 23, 1500, Francisco de Bobadilla arrived in Hispaniola. The first thing he saw were the dead bodies of seven Spaniards hanging from the gallows and five more waiting to be hanged. Columbus had found them all guilty of treason. Bobadilla was shocked. He did not even ask any questions. He simply arrested Columbus and ordered him to be taken back to Spain in chains. But no one had the courage to fasten the chains around the wrists and ankles of the Governor General, the Admiral of the Ocean Sea, and Viceroy of the Indies.

Finally Columbus's cook stepped forward and said he would do it. The admiral was put in chains and spent two months locked up in Hispaniola. Later the captain of the ship that took Columbus back to Spain offered to remove the chains, but Columbus refused. His pride was hurt and he insisted that only the queen herself could give the order to remove them.

Upon arriving in Spain, Columbus was taken to the royal court. In proud silence, he approached the king and queen with his heavy chains dragging behind him. The queen immediately ordered them removed. Columbus kept the chains because he felt they were a reminder that he had been specially chosen by God to open new lands to Christianity. Naturally he was in a rage about the

treatment he had received. He demanded that the king and queen return him to Hispaniola with full honors and punish Governor Bobadilla. Although they ordered Bobadilla to come home, the king and queen did not reappoint Columbus as governor of Hispaniola.

Columbus was now 50 years old. His hair was white and he was stiff with arthritis. He pleaded to the king and queen to give him one more chance. This time he would explore the western side of the Indies and find a passage through to the Indian Ocean.

The queen agreed. She gave Columbus four rickety ships and 135 men. But she laid down two rules: *not* to bring back any more slaves and *not* to land at Hispaniola. Columbus was to look for gold and stay out of trouble!

On May 9, 1502, Christopher Columbus set out for the fourth time. He called this trip his "High Voyage" and took along his younger son, Fernando, who was 13 at the time. On June 15, Columbus discovered an island later to be named Martinique. It was just south of Domenica, the island that was inhabited by cannibals. Two weeks later, he arrived off the coast of Hispaniola. As he came within sight of Santo Domingo, the chief settlement on the island, he noticed that the tide was rising. The winds were stronger and feathery clouds moved quickly across the sky. There was a heaviness in the air and Columbus could feel his arthritis acting up. To him all these signs meant one thing — a hurricane was brewing!

Columbus sent a message to the governor, asking for permission to enter the harbor. He also warned him that a hurricane was coming and advised that no ships leave the island. But the governor would not let Columbus enter the port and laughed at the warning. Fortunately he was able to find safety in a protected cove of another island. The next day, 30 Spanish ships set sail for Spain, carrying gold and other native goods. Columbus was furious over being refused shelter in the land he had won for Spain.

Out at sea, the governor's ships were struck by violent winds and waves. Ironically, the only ship to make it back to Spain was the one carrying Columbus's share of gold and his possessions from Hispaniola. Later the governor claimed that Columbus had performed black magic and caused the storm as revenge. Columbus himself regarded what had happened as a miraculous sign that God was on his side.

The hurricane was only the beginning of Columbus's latest troubles. As he sailed up and down the coast of Central America, rain, thunder, lightning and wind besieged his four ships. It was sheer luck that they escaped being destroyed by a huge waterspout that sucked up everything in its path.

Up and down the coast Columbus sailed, looking for a passage to the Indian Ocean. He often went ashore to ask natives about waterways across the land. Each time he followed their directions, but he failed to find a passage.

Finally the ships reached what is called Panama today. Central America is only 31 miles wide at one place in that country. Although Columbus did not know it, the Pacific Ocean was on the other side of that narrow strip of land. How surprised he would have been to find spread before him a vast body of water that led to the Indies.

As a result of the heat and wetness, the admiral's ships became infested with shipworms, which are a kind of clam that eats holes in wood. Columbus finally had to leave one of the ships behind because it was so badly weakened by the clams. The remaining ships were almost as bad, and the sailors had to bail them out night and day. Soon another ship had to be abandoned. Then a terrible storm hit the last two ships. They wallowed in the fierce waves while the crews bailed and pumped. On June 25, the ships limped into Jamaica, an island that Columbus had discovered on his second voyage. It lies off the southern coast of Cuba. Because the ships could no longer stay afloat, Columbus ran them up on the beach and built palm-thatched roofs over the decks.

Columbus spent the next year stranded in Jamaica. He was ill with malaria and had swollen joints from arthritis. In spite of his illnesses and the loss of his ships, he never gave up hope. Most of his time was spent trying to control the sailors and keeping peace with the natives who supplied them with food.

Finally, in July, a man named Diego Mendez was sent in a canoe to Hispaniola to bring help. But as the seasons passed and no ship arrived, Columbus was convinced that Diego had drowned.

It wasn't until June, 1504, almost two years later, that Diego returned from Hispaniola. It turned out that the governor had been in no hurry to help, claiming that he could not spare a ship any sooner. On June 28, Columbus and 100 men were taken to Santo Domingo on

Hispaniola. The Admiral of the Ocean Sea was now 53 years old and in poor health. As soon as he could, he chartered another ship and set sail for Spain.

He arrived there in November, 1504, and immediately tried to see the king and queen. But Queen Isabella was sick. She died three weeks after he arrived and Columbus was never able to see her. He had lost a true friend and his only real supporter.

Columbus himself was now so ill that he could not even get out of bed. But he was determined to collect all of the rewards he felt were owed to him. He sent many petitions to the king, who generally ignored them. Although Columbus had a great deal of money, he insisted that the amount was not as large as had been agreed upon. He also wanted the title of Governor of Hispaniola to be restored to him. King Ferdinand finally gave the title to Columbus's son Diego in 1508.

In his last days, Christopher Columbus tried to figure out why he had not come across more proof that he had reached the Indies. He still had no idea that the world was three times larger than he believed and that Japan was 10,000 miles beyond Europe; or that the Pacific Ocean existed and two continents stood between Europe and Asia. It never occurred to him that he had been lost in a New World.

John Cabot

Not much is known of John Cabot's childhood, but we do know that he was born Giovanni Caboto around the year 1451 in Genoa, which is located on the west coast of Italy. Christopher Columbus was born in the same year and in the same city. It is possible that they even knew each other as young boys.

When John was ten, his father took him to the city of Venice on the eastern coast of Italy. There he learned to read

and write. He also picked up the basics of navigation, which was done mainly by compass and the guidance of charts called *portolans*.

John became a seaman on one of the many-oared trading galleys that sailed to Beirut, Haifa and Alexandria. Today these cities are ports in Lebanon, Israel and Egypt. The galleys came home with their holds filled with silks, gold, ivory and spices that had been come overland by camel caravan from India. From the huge warehouses on the busy wharves of Venice, Italy, the goods were shipped by sea to Spain, France, and as far away as England.

In 1476, when Cabot was 26 years old, he obtained his papers as a citizen of Venice. It is likely that the merchants of Venice supported his application for cit-

izenship because he had a reputation as a good seaman and would probably make a fine commander of a trading vessel someday. Cabot was known for his great skill and courage in navigating the seas. Two years later, he was given command of his first galley. This was a great compliment, since the mariners of Venice were known as skilled and bold sailors.

For the next eight years, John Cabot traded with the eastern ports of the Mediterranean, gaining more and more experience with galleys. These ships used sails, but they were driven largely by oars. The crews, sometimes numbering 200, were mainly rowers. Each oar weighed about 120 pounds. Most rowers were criminals of some sort, and armed guards supervised, keeping a close watch on them.

As captain, Cabot spent a lot of time in his cabin. This allowed him to study the newest navigational charts.

PORTOLANS

Portolans were charts that mariners used to guide them in the sea. Coastlines were marked on these charts in black. Red flags indicated the important harbors. The portolans also had intersecting compass lines, which helped mariners chart a course. Maps with latitudes and longitudes came much later.

At the time, the Portuguese were pioneering in the exploration of the southern part of Africa. They believed that once they rounded the southern tip of that continent, they would be able to sail eastward to India and the Spice Islands. However, an Italian geographer named Paolo Toscanelli dal Pozzo had declared that Asia could be reached more quickly by sailing westward across the Ocean Sea.

As Cabot studied, he began to wonder which route would be shorter — eastward around Africa or westward across the Ocean Sea? He soon agreed with Toscanelli that westward was easier and quicker.

Cabot was well educated and did not believe any of the tales of the Ocean Sea being inhabited by sea monsters. He thought that crossing it depended entirely on the skill of the captain and soundness of his ship. Since he was a good seaman, Cabot was sure he could manage the voyage. Gradually this thought turned into his life's ambition — to captain his own ship across the Ocean Sea to the Far East. But it all seemed highly unlikely, since he lived in Venice, thousands of miles away from the Ocean Sea. Cabot knew that for such a voyage he would need friends in high places and the backing of a king.

One day John Cabot's employers of-

fered him a job in England. They wanted him to go to Bristol to buy cloth and wool. In turn he would sell silks, spices and beautiful Venetian glass. Cabot was not anxious to leave the beautiful, warm city of Venice for cold, gray England. But he thought that perhaps the move would lead him closer to his dream of crossing the Ocean Sea. It also occurred to him that English merchants would be interested in finding a short route to the Indies because their country happened to lie at the end of the spice route. This meant that the English paid the highest prices.

So Cabot went to the busy port of Bristol, then a bustling industrial city in southwest England. It is located on the Avon River. Downstream, the river widens into the Severn River and beyond that lies the vast Ocean Sea (Atlantic

Ocean). At least he would now be closer to his goal.

The Bristol merchants impressed Cabot. They were willing to take on any sound venture that might bring new profits. Besides trading with Spain, France and the Mediterranean countries, Bristol ships sailed northward to Ireland for wool and cattle. They even ventured into the wild North Atlantic to bring back cargos of codfish from Iceland.

John Cabot soon became well-known and liked in Bristol. The merchants regarded him as a good businessman who was also honest. Sailors respected him for his vast seamanship and for the fact that he had commanded ships himself. But most people had difficulty trying to pronounce Giovanni Caboto, so they began to call him the English version of his name — John Cabot.

Cabot was most impressed with the fact that the Bristol merchants had begun to explore the Ocean Sea. Like him, they did not fear it. Cabot soon longed to command one of their ships, but he knew that as a foreigner he had little chance. In addition, he was employed by Venetian merchants, not the English. So he kept his ambition to himself. Rather than push for his own ideas, Cabot was content to be measured by his actions.

Cabot continued to live in Bristol

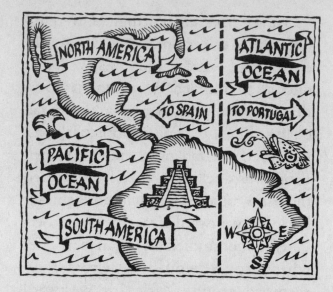

with his wife and three sons, doing business and always studying the newest maps and charts. During these years, he figured out that the shortest route across the Ocean Sea to China and Japan was a northern one along the 60th parallel. He happened to be almost right — the shortest route from England is a little south of his route. However, for ships the North American continent stands in the way.

In 1493, Columbus returned from his voyage of discovery on the western side of the Ocean Sea. He claimed that he had found the outlying islands of China and the Indies. Cabot decided he would do better than Columbus and reach the Indies by a shorter route.

Also in 1493, Pope Alexander VI set up a line running north and south on the map of the Ocean Sea to settle conflicts between Spain and Portugal arising out of Columbus's first voyage. The rights to all lands and seas lying west of the line were given to Spain; all lands and seas east of the line were given to Portugal. The agreement between the two rival countries was called the Treaty of Tordesillas.

The Bristol merchants were angry that England had been left out of the deal completely. They decided that they would carry on with their own voyages of exploration, but would stay in the North Atlantic. When they consulted Cabot on the matter, they were pleased to hear that he thought the quickest route to the Indies was a northern one. Like most people of the time, he thought that Columbus had found outlying islands of Cathay (China). Thus it seemed simple logic that the mainland must lie much farther to the north. The merchants approved of Cabot's theory.

John Cabot was now in his mid-forties, a respectable married man with children. He was tall with wide shoulders, a bearded face and a high forehead. He undoubtedly impressed the merchants as a man who could command a ship.

The charts Cabot had drawn himself were accurate and his astrolabe and compass, which had been made in Florence, were better instruments than the English captains used.

The Bristol merchants believed that John Cabot had the necessary knowledge for the task. He was also a good seaman and a greatly skilled navigator. To get royal backing, they sent a petition to King Henry VII (who ruled from 1485 to 1509). In it they requested "authority for John Cabot, citizen of Venice and his sons, Lewis, Sebastian and Santius, the royal grant of right under the king's banners, to discover and find whatever islands, countries, regions and provinces of the heathen and infidels in whatever part of the world they be, which before this time have been unknown to all Christians."

Simply stated, it meant that Cabot would have the right to seize any land inhabited by natives who were not Christian and had a different color skin. This was one way in which European monarchs added wealth to their nations.

King Henry VII was jealous of Columbus's recent discovery of new lands for Spain. When he received the petition from Bristol, he decided that he was not going to miss his chance to share the riches of the Far East. He was pleased that the merchants asked for no money to finance the expedition.

The English ruler wasted no time. In ten days the petition was granted. The king had added a single condition: Cabot had to give him one fifth of all the goods and treasures that he might find. Henry also gave Cabot full authority to sail to all countries and seas to the east, west and north. He did not mention the south because that meant he would be ignoring the Pope's edict. But he thought that if Cabot kept to the North Atlantic there would be less trouble with Spain, whose interests lay in the warmer seas to the south.

His sponsors provided Cabot with one small, 50-ton vessel named the *Mathew.* It was a good, solid ship with two masts, fast and quick to respond to the helm. The single deck swept upward to a high bow, which was necessary to plough through the treacherous North Atlantic waves.

From sailors familiar with Iceland, Cabot had learned that in the spring he would have more favorable winds for a westward crossing. On the morning of May 2, 1497, John Cabot took command of the *Mathew.* There was no flag waving as he sailed down the Avon River to the Ocean Sea. Aboard were 18 Bristol seamen. Their names are not known.

To reach what he thought was Japan (really the North American continent), Cabot chose to sail along the 60th parallel. However, he did not keep a record, or log, of his voyage. But we can imagine that after 30 days the sailors started to become anxious because Cabot had promised that their crossing would be shorter than Columbus's, which took 33 days.

On June 24, 1497, Cabot finally sighted land. Where this was no one really knows. After the sighting, he steered south, looking for a harbor. Somewhere along this 900-mile leg of his voyage, Cabot dropped anchor in a natural harbor. He rowed ashore with some of his crew and planted the royal flag of England and that of Venice on a stretch of grass.

There was no living person in sight. But Cabot did see signs of life. Several trees appeared to have been chopped down with an axe. Traps had been set to catch game and a sailor found a needle

reached a place off the coast of New-foundland where the water was very shallow and teeming with codfish. He later said, "The sea in these parts holds great quantities of fish, which may be taken merely by the lowering of a weighted basket into the water." This area became known as the Grand Banks, and is one of the finest fishing grounds in the world.

Cabot sailed on, finding and naming Cape Discovery, Saint George's Cape and the Trinity Islands. No one knows the exact locations of these places. They may have been in Labrador, Newfound-land or on Cape Breton Island. Wherever they were, Cabot later reported that the land was good for farming and the climate was mild.

Time ran out for Cabot and he headed the *Mathew* east toward home. It

that was probably used for weaving fishing nets. But Cabot did not explore inland. Perhaps he did not want to run into natives while he was too far from his ship for assistance. Or perhaps it was the swarms of large, hungry mosquitos that bred in the small pools of water on the rocky surface.

There were no brown-skinned natives like the ones Columbus had met, no golden rooftops, no great city of wealth, no silks, gold or precious stones. There was only the empty, rocky shore and the Ocean Sea to the east. Cabot did not know where he was, but he did know that it was "new-found land." The discovery later became known as Newfoundland, which is now part of Canada.

Cabot quickly pulled up the anchor and sailed the *Mathew* farther south. He is not known whether he doubled back along the same route he had come, or whether he headed straight out from his southernmost point across the wide Ocean Sea.

Cabot arrived back in England on August 6, 1497, sure that he had found some part of the Asian continent. But the merchants of Bristol were disappointed that he had not returned with gold, silks and spices. All he had to show for his trip was a needle and some traps. Cabot, however, was anxious to tell the king of his discoveries. Four days after his return, he presented King Henry VII with the chart he made of his voyage and the few tokens. The king was pleased, for he thought Cabot had claimed a part of Asia for England. Henry gave him 10 pounds, which is equivalent to several thousand dollars in modern currency. Although this was not much for the man who had supposedly found a new route to Asia, Cabot did not complain.

Cabot's discovery, which he claimed for England, created quite a stir among the ambassadors from other countries who lived in England. They sent off messages to their kings to report on Cabot's discovery of a part of Asia. The big fuss over Cabot impressed the king. A month later, he decided to pay the explorer 20 pounds every year and to provide assis-

tance for a second voyage.

Cabot was now held in very high esteem and people began to call him the "Great Admiral." Men all over England wanted to meet him and shake his hand.

On February 3, 1498, Henry VII issued the letters for Cabot's second voyage, granting him six ships and the authority to enlist English sailors. The plan was to sail along the coast from the place he found on the first voyage, and to sail west until he reached the shores of "China." There Cabot was to set up a colony and trading post. In the king's mind, London would become a more important trading center than Alexandria in Egypt.

With the king providing the financial support, merchants of Bristol and London supplied the ships, the provisions for

one year and large quantities of cloth, caps, laces and other trifles that natives were thought to like. Two hundred men volunteered for the voyage.

Only five ships were ready by May of 1498, when the winds were favorable for crossing the ocean. So Cabot left with fewer ships than planned. However, he soon ran into heavy storms. One vessel was badly damaged from the pounding and had to sail back to port. The other four ships held to their course and faded from sight across the stormy sea.

John Cabot's own name and reputation faded with them. Again Cabot kept no records of his voyage, and even today, after much research by historians, the details are incomplete. In England his second voyage was ignored because he brought back no news of interest or any

great treasures. In fact, he was forgotten so completely that it was the general belief that Cabot was lost at sea.

Although there is still some doubt about what happened to him, it is now believed that Cabot led his four ships to the east coast of Greenland. Hoping to find a shorter route to Asia, he led the little fleet north. His ships and men were not equipped for the icy cold seas and Cabot changed his course. He steered south, stopping briefly along the coast of Labrador (now part of Canada) and then headed down the coast until he sighted what is now Cape Cod, Massachusetts. The ships did not land, but continued

WHO REALLY DISCOVERED AMERICA?

Although John Cabot is credited with the discovery of North America, it had actually been visited hundreds of years earlier by Europeans from Scandinavia. Around the year 1000, the sea-roving Vikings had set up colonies in Iceland and Greenland. About 1010, the Viking Leif Eriksson sailed from Greenland down the coast of Canada and most likely landed in what is now the northeastern United States. He called this place Vinland, or "Wineland," because of the grapes he found there. Over the centuries that followed, however, the discoveries of the Vikings were forgotten by Europeans.

south until they reached a latitude of 38 degrees, near the entrance to the Chesapeake Bay. From there Cabot sailed for home. He returned without having found the rich shores of China. But he *had* discovered North America.

No doubt Cabot sailed home a disappointed man. Afterward King Henry VII and the English merchants lost all interest in the exploration of the North Atlantic. And John Cabot was forgotten. Later, Cabot's son Sebastian claimed the discovery of Newfoundland for himself because he said he had sailed with his father on his first voyage. But little credit has been given to Sebastian's claim.

Though not known at the time, John Cabot, lost in a "new-found land," had discovered North America. This was only six years after Columbus had stumbled upon the southern part of the same continent. Cabot's discovery was more valuable than all the gold, silver and jewels brought home by more famous explorers. It became the basis for England's claim to North America.

Eventually 13 British colonies would be established in the New World. Then, nearly three hundred years after Cabot's last voyage, those colonies would leave the mother country to become the new United States.

FERDINAND MAGELLAN

Ferdinand Magellan was born around 1480 in the rugged hills of northern Portugal. Early in his life, he spent a lot of time hunting the ferocious wolves and wild boars that roamed the hills where he lived. He was a tough and brave boy who often had to make quick decisions. This ability would come in handy when he grew up.

Ferdinand was lucky to be born into a noble family. At the age of 12, he was accepted as a page at the court of King John II of Portugal. Although he would have to live in Lisbon, far from home, this was expected of young boys from noble families. Life at court was very

nand was an ambitious young man and wanted to be part of the exciting voyages of discovery.

Unfortunately for him, King John II died in 1495 and the queen's brother, Manuel, became the king of Portugal. King Manuel I was not particularly interested in exploration and he did not like Ferdinand very much. Whenever the young man begged the king to let him go to sea, the king would refuse. Pages from families of more influence were given preference. In 1496, the king did raise him to the rank of squire, but he still would not give Ferdinand a position on any of the ships setting out to explore the unknown.

Then in 1497, Vasco da Gama sailed around the southern tip of Africa and reached the true Indies. He returned to Portugal with a fabulous cargo of treasures. Ferdinand could wait no longer to go to sea. Day after day he begged the king to let him go. But it seemed the more he begged, the more annoyed the king became. The king did, however, give Ferdinand a job helping to prepare ships for their voyages. But this only frustrated him even more.

For the next several years Ferdinand watched ships leave Lisbon and return filled with spices, silks, gold and other treasures. He worked very hard to prove

different from life in the hills. Dressed in the uniform of a page, Ferdinand carried the queen's flags and delivered messages to court officials. He also studied music, dancing, hunting and horsemanship.

King John II was interested in exploration and trade with other countries, so pages added astronomy, mapmaking and navigation to their studies. What Ferdinand liked best of all about his life at court was that he could see the distant ocean and sailing ships from the palace towers.

In 1493 Ferdinand heard the news that Christopher Columbus had sailed westward from Spain and reached the Indies (actually Central America). Bartolomeau Dias had already rounded the southern tip of Africa, opening up the eastern trade route to the Indies. Ferdi-

to the king that he was worthy of going to sea.

Portugal was becoming rich and powerful as a result of trade with the Indies. King Manuel was determined to prevent his country's traditional Moslem enemies (Egyptians, Turks and other peoples in the eastern part of the world) from regaining control over vital trading routes. In 1505, to protect his investments, he commissioned a large fleet of 22 ships to drive away Arab traders from the east coast of Africa and the surrounding seas. This would allow Portugal to bring the products of the Indies to Portugal by the new sea route.

Magellan begged to be allowed to leave court and join the fleet. This time King Manuel said yes. An ambitious young man like Magellan would be a good person to have on such an expedition. Finally at about the age of 25, Magellan felt the swell of the Ocean Sea (Atlantic Ocean) beneath his feet.

First he patrolled the east coast of Africa, helping to protect Portuguese bases from there. As a young officer, he participated in the sinking of many Arab ships. He was then sent to India. Magellan fought fearlessly in naval battles against Arabs, Egyptians, Indians and Turks. He was wounded in 1506 while helping to defeat a large fleet of 100

enemy ships near the port of Diu on the west coast of India.

Magellan had hardly recovered from his wounds when he was sent on another expedition to strengthen Portuguese control of the Far East. His ship sailed to Malacca, a port in Malaya that the Portuguese wanted for their own purposes. When they arrived, the harbor was filled with Chinese, Malay and Arab ships. It was obvious that the Portuguese were not wanted because every cannon in Malacca was pointing at them. The Portuguese quickly reversed course and sailed out of the harbor.

On the return voyage to India, Magellan's ship was attacked by Chinese pirates. Magellan led a counterattack and almost single-handedly captured the Chinese ship.

When the Portuguese returned to Lisbon, the king rewarded Magellan by making him captain of his own ship. Eager to prove himself even more, Magellan joined an expedition in 1511 and fought during the Portuguese capture of Malacca.

Magellan, however, was much more interested in exploration than fighting, and he sailed to the Spice Islands (the Moluccas). From there he sailed beyond the limits of the known world and discovered what would become known as the Philippine Islands.

After eight years in the Far East, Magellan returned to Portugal in 1512. He had expected to return to honor and fame. After all, he had shown great courage and had displayed a unique ability to act quickly under fire. He knew the East better than most men of his time and had become one of the world's most skillful navigators.

Magellan, however, returned to Portugal only to wind up in hot water because of his frank opinions. The reason for his trouble was the Treaty of Tordesillas, an agreement between Spain and Portugal that cut the world in two with an imaginary line running north to south in the western Atlantic. This line had been drawn in 1493 by Pope Alexander VI to settle territorial disputes between the two countries. As a result, Spain claimed all newly discovered lands and seas west of this line, and Portugal claimed all lands and seas east of this line. Of course, it did not matter to either country that those lands might be inhabited by people who thought they were the rightful owners.

The big question to be decided was where the line ran on the far side of the globe. No one knew for sure because the exact circumference of the world was unknown. Thus it was impossible to measure halfway around the globe when the distance all the way around was a mystery.

Magellan, who always spoke what was on his mind, told the king that he thought the Philippine Islands were so far around to the east of the globe that they probably came within the Spanish half. This was not what King Manuel wanted to hear. Even though he was obliged to abide by the Treaty of Tordesillas, Spain was their arch rival. The king was outraged by such opinions and called Magellan a traitor, stripping him of his command.

Magellan was desperate to regain King Manuel's trust so that he could captain another ship on a voyage back to the East. Since the Portuguese were gradually subduing all the ports on the continent's western seacoast, there were plenty of battles to be fought. Hoping to gain the king's attention, Magellan volunteered for an expedition against rebellious tribes in North Africa. He fought bravely and was badly wounded in the knee, which caused him to limp for the rest of his life. To make matters worse, he was accused of stealing some of the booty captured in battle. Now he did get the king's attention, but not the kind he wanted.

Magellan may have been a stubborn and prickly sort of fellow, but he was not dishonest. Eventually the charges against him were dropped. And once again he pleaded with the king to give him command of a ship. But King Manuel only called him "clubfoot" and refused to see him.

Two years passed without a promotion or a job in the service of the king, who refused to even talk with Magellan. Then Magellan took a rash step. He sneaked his name onto a list of commoners who were to be received publicly by the king. When "Magellan" was called, there was a quiet stir among the people of the court. No one of noble birth ever stooped so low as to appear among commoners seeing the king. But Magellan limped forward and knelt before the throne. First he asked for a promotion

and then for a ship to command. The king was so angry that he told Magellan that there was no place for him at all in the Portuguese fleet.

This time Magellan was completely humiliated. He left Lisbon around 1516 and fled up the coast to the town of Oporto. There he lived almost like a hermit, hardly ever going out and speaking only to a few men who had once been in the service of the king. It was a difficult time for Magellan, but it was in Oporto that he worked out a plan to reach the Spice Islands by sailing west rather than east.

It had become clear by this time that Columbus had not found a route to the Indies. The discoveries of explorers like Amerigo Vespucci, who landed on the coast of Brazil, showed that Columbus had discovered a new world — the continent and islands of South America. But everything between this large continent and Asia was still a big mystery. Mapmakers knew that there was an ocean, which they called the South Sea or Eastern Ocean (the Pacific Ocean), but they had no idea how big it was.

Magellan's problem was how to sail around the new continent into what Europeans called the South Sea (the Pacific Ocean). In 1511, John of Lisbon had led an expedition to Rio de la Plata, a river in what is now Argentina. He thought that the river was a passage, or strait, that cut westward through South America to the East Indies. However, he had not sailed through it. Magellan decided that he would find the strait of John of Lisbon and sail on to the Indies. If King Manuel did not want his service, perhaps King Charles I of Spain would.

In 1517 Magellan was invited to Seville, Spain, by Diego Barbosa, a successful Portuguese captain who lived there. They made plans for an expedition to be sponsored by the king and commanded by Magellan, who was now in his late thirties. The purpose was to find John of Lisbon's passage to the Spice Islands. King Charles I of Spain was very impressed when Magellan said, "I will find a new route to the East by sailing west." He showed the king a hand-painted globe made of leather. Then he pointed to the Spice Islands (the Moluccas), a small cluster in the midst of the East Indies. No European country yet controlled them. And Magellan was sure they were in the Spanish half of the world.

Since the only known sea route to the Indies was around Africa by way of the Cape of Good Hope, which was in the Portuguese zone, the king was eager to find an alternate route. But he was not so sure it could be done. Magellan pointed to the globe where it showed a strait, called "El Paso," leading from the Atlantic to the Great South Sea. "I know of a secret passage that I will find," he told the king. He also said that he would reach the Philippine Islands by sailing in the opposite direction of his first voyage to that part of the world.

What Magellan proposed was a voyage of thousands of miles, lasting two years. It would link the two halves of the known world. King Charles quickly agreed. A successful voyage would give Spain a share of the spice trade and allow him to claim the Philippines. He appointed Magellan as captain-general of the expedition. The money to pay for everything was put up by three men (financiers) who would receive a large share of the profits from a successful voyage.

Magellan finally felt liked and appreciated. He now had a wife, a son, many new friends, and he was the captain-general of a five-ship fleet about to set off on a major voyage of exploration. His dreams seemed to be coming true. Magellan soon discovered, however, that he had many enemies.

King Manuel I of Portugal regarded the Spice Islands as his property and he was unhappy about Magellan working for his arch-rival. So he sent agents to steal the expedition's supplies and stop the fleet from sailing. Meanwhile, the three financiers were not at all interested in exploration. Their goal was to become rich through a shorter route to the Spice Islands. So they persuaded the king to let them choose the captains of the ships. They named three out of the five captains and appointed other men in important positions. They all had the same goals in mind: get to the Spice Islands as quickly as possible, fill their holds with profitable goods and sail back as quickly as possible. They would be in conflict with the captain-general at almost every stage of the voyage.

The flagship that Magellan captained was the *Trinidad*. The *San Antonio*, *Concepción* and *Victoria* were captained by men named Cartegena, Quesada and Mendoza. The smallest ship was the *Santiago* and its captain was named Serrano, the only captain who was a friend of Magellan. A total of 265 men signed up for the voyage.

A two-year expedition required a huge amount of food and supplies: 100 tons of sea biscuits, 32 tons of salted beef, and 26 tons of salted pork, as well as cheese, beans, rice, onions, flour, water and wine. For repairing the ships they needed lumber, nails, canvas and tar. To defend themselves against the Portuguese

and hostile natives, they equipped the ships with 58 cannons, 5,000 pounds of gunpowder, 1,000 lances and hundreds of swords, arrows, crossbows, javelins and suits of armor. The trade goods included copper bars, bracelets, knives, scissors, mirrors, fake jewels, fishhooks and colored cloth. These items were known to be popular with the merchants in the Spice Islands.

Finally, on September 20, 1519, the fleet set sail and headed into the Atlantic. Magellan led the fleet south. He ordered the other ships to follow his lead. At night he lit a *farol*, which is a large torch, so they could see him.

Seven days into the voyage, the fleet reached Tenerife, one of the Canary Islands, a group off the northwest coast of

Africa. There Magellan found out that the Spanish captains were planning to kill him. They tried to cause an argument with Magellan, hoping to start a fight that would lead to his death. But the captain-general remained calm and acted as if he did not know what they were trying to do.

As Magellan led the fleet south along the African coast, large fish swam alongside of the ships. The sailors recognized them as sharks, with their terrible teeth and their reputation for devouring shipwrecked sailors. The sharks followed the ships for a while, as if hoping for a meal. When the fleet neared the equator, it was pounded by thunderstorms and huge waves. Naturally the crews were scared. They had just set out on a two-year journey and already their lives were in danger.

Then the ships were battered by violent electrical storms, which caused a strange effect known as "Saint Elmo's Fire." It made the masts glow and flicker with a ghostly light. The sailors knew nothing of electricity and they believed the light meant that Saint Elmo, patron saint of seamen, was protecting them. This calmed their fears, at least for a while.

After being lashed by high winds and heavy rains, the ships drifted into the doldrums, an area of calms and sudden storms near the equator. There was no wind to fill the sails and for over three weeks the ships stayed almost motionless in the flat calm of the sea. The sun blazed down and the intense heat melted the tar between the ships' timbers. The hulls began to leak. Water and wine barrels burst and the food went rotten.

Gradually the ocean currents carried the ships out of the doldrums and the sails filled again. Magellan set their course southwest. When the fleet sailed past the equator, the North Star disappeared below the horizon because the curvature of the earth was in the way. So Magellan learned to navigate by the brighter stars and constellations south of the equator. However, his captains did not like losing sight of the North Star, which was basic to their navigation.

On the crossing, Captain Cartegena argued with Magellan about which course to take. But this time he organized a mutiny. Magellan had him arrested and put in chains, which restored order for the moment.

The fleet sighted land near what is now Recide, Brazil, on November 29, 1519. Magellan continued south, and in early January the ships anchored in what is now known as Rio de Janeiro. This means "River of January," and it was named for the month in which it was discovered. The blue bay stands out against green mountains, and it is one of the most beautiful harbors in the world.

It was summertime in countries south of the equator and there had been a two-month drought in the area. It came to an end just as the fleet arrived, and the natives thought that the white men were gods who had brought the rain. Magellan was very friendly to them. He traded mirrors, knives and fishhooks, and in turn the natives provided chickens, fish, potatoes and sweet pineapples, along with live parrots and monkeys.

Magellan and his crews spent 13 days resting, repairing the storm damage to the ships and taking on fresh water and food. On Christmas Day, the fleet set sail again. Full of hope, Magellan led the ships down the coast of South America. Although most of the continent was still unknown, Portuguese and Spanish geographers estimated that it was about the same size and shape as Africa and that it was in approximately the same position north and south of the equator. Magellan was sure that he was close to finding "El Paso."

On January 11, 1520, the fleet reached a point where the coast seemed to swing to the west as far as the eye could see, just as John of Lisbon had described it. When the ships entered a broad, open channel,

Magellan called his crews together. "El Paso!" he cried, convinced that he had found it. He told the sailors that they were about to enter seas where no Christian had ever sailed before.

The captain-general sent the *Santiago* to follow the coast and explore "El Paso." He sailed southward in the *Trinidad* with the others. Now Magellan was certain that he would locate the large land mass that was believed to exist beyond the tip of South America.

A few days later the fleet assembled again, but there was only bad news. Magellan had not found the land mass. Worse yet, the *Santiago* reported that the Rio de la Plata was not "El Paso" at all. It was only a great river emptying into the sea. Magellan refused to believe this. If it were true, the whole purpose of his journey was meaningless. He led the fleet into the channel to see for himself. Even when the water became too shallow for the ships to navigate, he refused to turn back. Instead Magellan had a longboat lowered over the side and was rowed westward. After three weeks, he had to admit that the river was not a passage through the continent leading to the East Indies. Today the Rio de la Plata is a major commercial waterway, providing seaports for both Uruguay and Argentina.

Stubborn as ever, Magellan refused to

give up his search for a passage to the Pacific Ocean. But the sailors were not as anxious to sail into uncharted regions. Who knew what they would run into? They urged Magellan to return to Rio de Janeiro for the winter. At least, it would be warmer there. Convinced that there was a strait only a few miles to the south, Magellan would not give in. The promise of riches was enough to persuade the sailors to continue the voyage.

So, in early February, the fleet left the Rio de la Plata and turned south again, into the unknown. The ships hugged the coast, exploring every inlet, bay and river mouth. As they sailed farther and farther south, they ran into some of the stormiest seas in the world. The wind was sometimes so strong that it actually drove the ships backward! Soon the temperature dropped below the freezing point. Thick ice formed on the masts and rigging, making the vessels top-heavy. They were in danger of capsizing in the rough seas.

For eight weeks the fleet battled the dangerous waters. Magellan always led the way in the *Trinidad.* They sailed over 1,000 miles along the coast of what is now Argentina. The sailors began to drop from exhaustion and cold. Finally, Magellan realized that they could go no farther and began to search for a sheltered place to spend the winter.

On March 31, 1520, the fleet headed into a natural harbor, which they called the Port of San Julian. It was a cold, lonely place surrounded by gray cliffs, not at all like the warm, lush green of Rio de Janeiro. Many of the crew members no longer believed in Magellan and his search for John of Lisbon's "El Paso." Surely, it did not exist. But they knew that they had sailed farther south than any other explorers before them. They thought that if they went any farther south, fierce storms might prevent them from ever turning back.

The three treacherous Spanish captains had finally had enough. They planned to mutiny and sail their ships back home as soon as the weather allowed. Just before midnight on April 1, thirty men led by Cartegena and

Quesada boarded and captured the *San Antonio*. By morning Magellan realized that something was wrong because the officers aboard the *San Antonio*, *Concepción* and *Victoria* refused to obey his orders. He acted swiftly and boldly. Pretending to negotiate with the mutineers, he sent a man named Espinoza with a letter to Mendoza, the captain of the *Victoria*. Espinoza gave Mendoza the letter with one hand and stabbed him to death with the other. At the same time, a group of Magellan's loyal crew swarmed aboard the *Victoria* and captured her.

Magellan immediately blockaded the entrance to the harbor with the three ships. He outmaneuvered the *San Antonio* and *Concepción*, and their captains surrendered. The mutiny was over.

The trial of the mutineers lasted five days. Magellan ordered Cartagena to be put in chains and to be marooned on shore. Quesada was beheaded. The bodies of Quesada and Mendoza were hung on posts around the bay at San Julian. The rest of the mutineers were put in chains. This left no doubt that Magellan was in command.

Now there was much work to be done. The loyal crew members built huts to sleep in and to store supplies. The mutinous crew members had the much more unpleasant job of "careening." This was done by beaching the ships at high tide and rolling them over on their sides. The mutinous sailors were kept in chains and worked waist-deep in freezing water, scraping barnacles from the hulls. They also replaced rotten timbers and sealed the seams with boiling tar.

While the ships were being unloaded, Magellan discovered that there was very little food left. He immediately set the men to work hunting, trapping and fishing. They found some very strange creatures to eat. There were black and white "goslings" that didn't fly, and "sea wolves" with large teeth and no legs. They were penguins and seals. Magellan's men had never seen such creatures before.

While the sailors were wondering at the strange animals, an even stranger sight appeared on the shore — a man who stood 7 1/2 feet tall. He wore animal skins that covered his body and feet. His face was painted red and his hair was painted white. The man danced and sang while throwing dust on his head. Was this the giant's way of saying hello? Magellan sent one of his crew members ashore to do exactly what the giant did as a sign of friendship. The giant pointed up to the sky, believing that Magellan and his men had come from there.

Magellan gave the giant food and some trinkets. Then he showed him a mirror, and when the man looked at his reflection, he became terrified. He had obviously never seen his reflection before, and he jumped back, knocking three sailors to the ground.

A few days later, more giants appeared, men and women, although the women were shorter and fatter. Magellan called these people "Patagonians" (from the Spanish word for "big feet"). This referred to the fact that they wrapped their feet in animal skins stuffed with straw. Magellan was friendly to them at first, but then he made the mistake of trying to capture two of the giants to take back to Spain. There was a fight, during which one of the crew members was killed. The giants managed to escape from the ships.

Magellan knew that he had lost the trust of these people and feared they might attack the expedition. He immediately sent the *Santiago* farther south to find new winter quarters. But the small ship ran into a storm and was wrecked in the mouth of the Santa Cruz River. Two of the survivors made their way back to San Julian for help. Magellan had no choice now but to spend the rest of the winter at Santa Cruz. Luckily, the giants never appeared again.

In August, 1520, the fleet put out to sea and headed south along the coast. The ships were now very close to the South Pole, in seas where storms can occur at any time. In fact, every day was stormy, dark and cold.

Then, on October 21, a cape was sighted through the clouds and mist. Magellan named it the Cape of Eleven Thousand Virgins (Cape Virgenes). Beyond the cape was a bay. The crews were sure that the bay led nowhere and was closed on all sides. Magellan, however, would not give up that easily. He sent the *San Antonio* and *Concepción* to discover what was inside the bay. Suddenly a storm blew up. Magellan's ship and the *Victoria* were tossed about mercilessly, but they managed to ride out the storm.

The *San Antonio* and the *Concepción* could not get back to the cape because a strong head wind drove them farther into the bay. Snow swept across the water and the crews panicked, fearing they would be crushed against the jagged rocks that lined the bay. The ships were blown back to the end of the bay, where they saw what seemed to be a small inlet. Desperate for safety, they entered it and to their surprise discovered a long waterway. There was land on both sides, and the saltiness of the water and the tides proved that it was not a river.

In fact, it was what they had been looking for — a deep-water strait that ran west. They followed "El Paso" into a bay, then into another strait and then another bay. Joyfully they turned back to tell the captain-general.

After 48 hours the storm ended. Magellan sailed the *Trinidad* close to the rocky shore, looking for any sign of wreckage or survivors. He was sure that the two ships had been thrown against the rocks and wrecked. Suddenly his lookout cried, "A sail!" Coming around the bay were the *San Antonio* and *Concepción*, their flags flying and the crews jumping and waving with joy on the decks. Magellan realized they had found "El Paso" at last. It wasn't anywhere near where John of Lisbon thought it was, but that didn't matter now.

Magellan proudly led his fleet through the deep and narrow passage we know now as the Strait of Magellan, near the tip of South America. The four ships sailed slowly past towering, snow-covered mountains and vast glaciers. They fought against fierce winds and constant squalls. Lines were frozen and the decks were covered with ice.

During the navigation of the strait, the new captain of the *San Antonio* became terrified that Magellan was leading the fleet to destruction. He waited for a dark night, then turned his ship and fled eastward through the strait back to Spain. Now the fleet was down to three ships.

After one month and 360 miles, they passed through the strait on November 28, 1520, and entered the Great South Sea (the Pacific Ocean). Magellan called his men together for a service of thanksgiving and solemnly named the body of water, "*Mar Pacifico*"(Peaceful Sea).

Magellan led the fleet northwest as quickly as possible to escape the freezing weather that resulted from being so close to the South Pole. When the ships finally reached the equator, Magellan turned westward. According to his estimation, the Pacific Ocean was about 600 miles wide. He was sure that they would be in the Spice Islands in three or four days.

Days passed, then weeks, and the voyage went on. December ended and the year 1521 arrived. A mild but steady breeze drove the ships across the ocean, but the horizon remained empty. Not a single island had been sighted, except for two tiny, uninhabited ones. The sailors became anxious and Magellan tried to figure out if his calculations were wrong. Where were the Spice Islands, or the Philippines? Could he be lost in this vast sea?

It didn't take Magellan long to realize that this sea was not as small as he thought. But every day he said, "Soon we will find land." The fact is that Magellan's Mar Pacifico is the largest ocean on earth, covering about one-third of the total surface of the planet.

As the days passed, the fleet's food supply began to run out. Under the intense sun of the tropics, the little they had

began to rot and their water turned yellow with bacteria. The starving sailors even ate the maggots that crawled in the rotting biscuits and drank the yellow slime that settled in the water barrels. They ate rats, sawdust, the leather from the rigging, and even their own boots!

Then the crews became sick with scurvy, caused by lack of vitamin C. Their arms and legs swelled, their gums turned blue and their teeth fell out. Horrible sores broke out on their bodies and they grew so weak that they could hardly man the sails. And one by one, they began to die. But Magellan kept the fleet turned to the west. He would reach the East Indies even if he had to sail the *Trinidad* by himself.

Finally on March 6, 1521, the lookout stationed in the *Trinidad*'s masthead thought he saw something. "Land! Land!" he cried, "Praise be to God!" On the horizon appeared a cluster of islands. As the ships drew nearer, the men were frantic with joy. Dark-skinned natives gathered in excited groups on the shore. Jumping into their canoes, they paddled out to the anchored ships and swarmed aboard. Seeing that the men were weak and sick, the natives stole everything they could lay their hands on.

Magellan and his crew fought them off with crossbows and fired a few shots from the cannons. The natives quickly retreated in fear. With every last bit of strength they had, the sailors made a quick landing and took as much food and water as they could and then quickly set sail. Magellan named the cluster the Ladrones Islands (Thieves Islands). Today they are known as the Marianas.

The captain-general had no idea where he was. He had, in fact, crossed over 8,000 miles of the Pacific Ocean and had reached one of the Mariana Islands, 1,250 miles east of the Philippines. On March 16, ten days later, the tiny fleet sighted another island. Magellan did not know it, but he had finally reached the Philippines. He landed on a small, uninhabited island, a beautiful place with sandy beaches, palm trees and abundant with fish, coconuts and other tropical fruits. Here the sailors rested and recovered from their long journey.

On March 28, 1521, the ships sailed to a small, inhabited island. The natives came alongside the ships in canoes. When Magellan listened to them talk, he realized that he was back in the islands he had visited many years before — the Philippines. This was a personal triumph. On his first visit, he had reached these islands by sailing east from Portugal. Now he had reached them by sailing west, as he had set out to do. Taking the two voyages together, he was the first man to have traveled all the way around the world!

Later that day, two large canoes came toward the *Trinidad*. The local king was in the larger one, seated under an awning. He did not come aboard. Magellan sent some presents to him and the king offered him a bar of gold and some ginger in return. The captain-general did not take the gifts. But the next day he sent his interpreter ashore to ask the king for food. The king, or raja, was named Colambu, and came himself with an escort of warriors. When he stepped aboard Magellan's ship, he embraced the captain-general and gave him fish, rice and fruits. Magellan gave the king a red-and-yellow shirt and a red cap. He showed the king other things like linen cloth and knives, mirrors and cannons and told him he would like to be his friend. The king agreed.

After that, King Colambu and Magellan actually became quite close. Magellan even converted him and some of his people to Christianity. Although the sailors were happy to trade their trinkets with the islanders for gold, they soon became anxious to leave for the Spice Islands, which were the next stop in their voyage. The captain-general, however, seemed to be losing interest in exploration. In fact, he became determined to convert the natives to Christianity, and he would use force if he had to.

There were still many treacherous officers among the ships' crews, and they became quite upset over this latest development. It was bound to keep them from reaching the Spice Islands for some time.

On April 7, Magellan led the fleet to Cebu, the wealthiest and most populous island in the Philippines. He had decided to claim all the islands for Spain. Cebu had many villages and many people. Magellan became friends with the raja, named Humabon, and they traded many goods. The ships took on gold, pearls, silks and gems in exchange for iron, copper, mirrors, scissors and knives.

The raja, his queen and the natives were converted to Christianity. Magellan

ordered a large cross to be erected on the shore and an altar to be built. The raja and thousands of his people were baptized by Catholic priests who had sailed with the expedition. Magellan was now on his way to making the Philippines, with its high volcanic islands, forests, blue water and brown people, into an outpost for Christian Spain.

The chiefs of neighboring villages and islands were all converted, except for one. When the Raja of Cebu told Magellan that King Cilapulapu, a powerful chieftain of the small island of Mactan, refused to become a Christian, the captain-general decided that the stubborn ruler must be punished.

He sent Espinoza with a party of men to attack Cilapulapu's island. They raided and burned down the main city

and killed many native men. Even so, the chieftain would not give in to Magellan's demands.

The captain-general was now determined to overcome Cilapulapu, even though his officers said it was too risky. He was on a crusade and seemed to have lost his senses. When he announced that he would lead another attack on Mactan and asked for volunteers, none of the experienced officers and fighting men responded. Raja Colambu offered to send one thousand warriors, but Magellan refused. He was convinced God would help him win the battle.

At midnight on April 26, Magellan and about 60 of his servants, stewards and seamen, rowed ashore to launch a surprise attack. But Cilapulapu and 3,000 islanders were waiting for them. When Magellan ordered his men to attack, they fired their crossbows and ad-

vanced forward. But the captain-general saw that they were being lured too far from their boats and ordered his men to retreat. They rushed for the boats, but Magellan was held back by his limp and was left behind with about 12 others.

For almost an hour, they held off the attacking natives. None of the other sailors came to help. Magellan was finally overpowered and driven back into the water, where he was stabbed to death.

This was what the rebellious Spanish officers had been waiting for. They immediately sent boats to rescue the four remaining men, but no one tried to recover the captain-general's body. With Magellan dead, the profit-hungry officers could now proceed to the Spice Islands. There they could fill their ships with goods that would make them and their financial backers rich. Hoping to destroy evidence of their treachery, they burned Magellan's logs. But they didn't know that there was one man named Pigafetta who kept a diary of the voyage. This would come back to haunt them.

There were now only ll5 men left out of the 277 who had set out from Spain. There were not enough to sail the three ships, so the *Concepción* was sunk. An officer named Carvalho took charge and the *Trinidad* and the *Victoria* set out to sea. But without Magellan's strong leadership, the Spaniards became a band of pirates, attacking unarmed trading ships and stealing their cargoes. After four months, Carvalho was deposed and a man named Espinoza took command. He ended the piracy and resumed the search for the Spice Islands, or Moluccas. At every island he reached, he asked directions. Finally, on November 8, 1521, the much-reduced fleet landed at Tidore, one of the Spice Islands.

Now the most profitable trading could take place. The sailors were so greedy that they overloaded the *Trinidad* with spices, silks, gold and precious gems. The cargo was so heavy that the ship sprang leaks. Espinoza remained behind with half of the men to repair the *Trinidad.* He ordered the *Victoria* to sail on to Spain under the command of Sebastian de Elcano. It left on February 21, 1522.

When the *Trinidad* was repaired, it sailed on toward Spain and was promptly captured by a Portuguese fleet. The *Victoria,* however, managed to avoid the Portuguese, who controlled all the ports on the eastern side of the world, and sailed through the Indian Ocean and around the Cape of Good Hope.

On September 6, 1522, three years after Magellan had set sail, the *Victoria* dropped anchor in the Bay of Sanlúcar in southern Spain. The ship had traveled more than 42,000 miles, over 21,800 of them while the little fleet was led by Magellan in waters never before sailed by Europeans. Of the 277 men who had started out, only 18 had survived. They were the first men to sail around the world in a single voyage.

Pigafetta was one of the crew members who made it back. He travelled throughout Europe, presenting kings and queens with excerpts from his log. It was first published in 1525, and from then on the account of Magellan's historic voyage and the treachery of his captains became well-known.

Ferdinand Magellan added greatly to the knowledge of the world, proving that it was possible to sail around South America. He showed beyond any doubt that the world was round and much larger than anyone believed. Although he had set out to discover a short route westward to the Spice Islands, his route was too long and too hazardous to be used. And eventually, after much arguing, it was shown that the Philippines lay on the Portuguese side of the line established in the Treaty of Tordesillas. Thus Magellan had been wrong when he told King Manuel I that the Spanish controlled the Philippines.

Wrong or not, Magellan had been

driven by a burning desire to explore the unknown. Lost along the coast of South America and in the vast Pacific Ocean, many men would have given up. But

Magellan had courage and stubbornness and his voyage of discovery turned out to be one of the greatest of all time.

GIOVANNI DA VERRAZANO

Giovanni da Verrazano was born around 1480. As a child he lived in Lyons, France. His real home, however, was the city of Florence in Italy. Verrazano's father had learned the silk-weaving trade as a young man in Florence and brought his family to Lyons, France, where there was a great demand for his trade. Many skilled and well-educated Florentines also lived in Lyons. Verrazano's father owned three small factories, in which raw silk from the Far East was woven into beautiful material. The silk produced by the factories was in constant demand by wealthy people.

Unlike many Florentines, Giovanni and his brother, Gierolomo, were not interested in business. Gierolomo was good at drawing and liked to make maps. Giovanni was a restless youth, and wanted to travel. When Giovanni was ten, the family went to Florence to visit his grandparents. Giovanni wished he could remain in Florence. It was an exciting and splendid city full of merchants, bankers, industrialists, artists and architects. When he returned to Lyons, Giovanni could not wait to leave and head south again to Florence.

As Giovanni grew older and the silk looms of Lyons clattered away in the factories, he made frequent trips to Italy to visit his grandparents. There he heard of the voyages of Christopher Columbus, who sailed across the great Ocean Sea (the Atlantic Ocean); of Vasco da Gama, who discovered a sea route to India; and of another Florentine, Amerigo Vespucci, who believed Columbus had not discovered the eastern shores of China, but rather another continent altogether.

Educated people all over Italy were excited by the new discoveries. To young men throughout Europe, explorers were the heroes of the age. Many, especially those from poor families, looked at voyages of exploration as a way to win fame and fortune. Giovanni had heard all the exciting stories and, at about 17, he decided he wanted to go to sea. He learned that there was a school in Florence where, among many other subjects, young men could receive training in the art of navigation. After they qualified, they became merchant sea captains.

From the time he was 18 until he was 21, Verrazano lived in Florence and studied the classics, higher mathematics, and navigation. Later Gierolamo went to school there, but he decided to become a geographer.

Before he was 22 years old, Verrazano went to sea as a junior officer on a Genoese galley. A year later, he was given command of his own galley. It was propelled by oars, but had a great triangular sail for use when the wind was favorable. Although the craft was not very seaworthy, it taught Giovanni all the finer points of sailing.

Giovanni was a silent and serious fellow who did not make many friends and never married. He spent most of his time learning all he could about the world, studying the latest information on newly discovered lands. He wanted to bring honors to Florence and perhaps increase business for the Florentine settlement of Lyons.

As captain of his own galley, Verrazano sailed to Alexandria, Beirut and Tyre (North African ports on the Mediterranean Sea). There he took on cargoes of raw silk, spices and incense, which he carried to ports in Italy, France and Spain. Of course, these goods came originally from China, the Spice Islands and India. They were transported by a route through the Persian Gulf and Red Sea and then by caravan to ports on the eastern Mediterranean. The silk was in great demand by wealthy people. And every household needed the spices to improve the taste of badly preserved meat. Business was good, and as the years passed Giovanni was promoted to a larger trading vessel.

By the year 1511, when Verrazano was around 31, navigators had explored almost the entire length of South America. Portuguese seamen had discovered a sea route to the Spice Islands (the Moluccas) and were on their way to complete domination of the Indian Ocean. In fact, they were cutting off the ability of other European countries to trade in the Persian Gulf. Verrazano soon began to feel the effects of their activities. By 1518, he could no longer purchase spices in Alexandria or Beirut. The Portuguese had so much influence that most of the spices were carried in Portuguese vessels.

With each voyage, Verrazano's problems increased. First there were no spices available. Then raw silk became impossible to find. With their supplies of raw materials dwindling, the merchants of Florence and Lyons became alarmed. Once-busy factories were forced to close. The only raw silk now came from Portugal, and the merchants of Lisbon were

demanding very high prices.

Verrazano was convinced that the Atlantic Ocean would be the new spice and silk route in the future. The country that found the route would be able to trade directly with the sources of those products. Verrazano was eager to prove his theory in a voyage of exploration. He and Gierolamo carefully studied a chart of the Atlantic Ocean prepared by a famous geographer named Apianus. The chart showed the outline of the east coast of what is now South America and the many islands and mainland coasts of the Caribbean. But the east coast of North America was made up of broken lines and lots of scattered islands, for very little exploration had actually taken place there.

Then, in 1522, the only surviving ship

of Magellan's fleet landed in Spain, having circumnavigated the globe. Magellan had proved that it was possible to reach the Spice Islands by sailing west. However, his passage to the Pacific Ocean through the southern tip of the South American continent was too far down the coast to be practical. The two Verrazano brothers discussed the possibility of an unknown channel lying much farther to the north than Magellan's strait, leading to China and the Spice Islands. They visited King Francis I of France in the royal palace and discussed their theory with him. Verrazano believed that this passage would allow European ships to reach the Spice Islands in ten days. The king was fascinated. He was convinced of Giovanni's enormous knowledge of seafaring matters and impressed by the accurate information that both brothers provided on other explorers' discoveries.

The king was eager to enter the race for the spice trade with the Portuguese and Spaniards, yet he was hesitant to sponsor the voyage Giovanni proposed. Such a plan would arouse the anger of Spain and Portugal. According to the Treaty of Tordesillas, he would be trespassing on Spanish and Portuguese territories. Finally, the king decided to forget about the treaty. After all, the French ignored it by fishing far out in the Atlan-

tic. English mariners also fished and traded throughout the North Atlantic.

King Francis finally decided to give Verrazano four ships. Florentine businessmen and a few wealthy Frenchmen provided the financing for the expedition. In the spring of 1523, Verrazano was ready to sail. But wild gales in the Atlantic Ocean prevented his departure. In May the weather began to improve and the order was given to sail. Led by Verrazano in the *Dauphine*, the smallest of the fleet, the four ships edged out of the harbor of Dieppe and headed for the gray emptiness of the ocean. Suddenly a tremendous gale came sweeping out of the west. The ships fought to stay afloat in the towering waves. The *Dauphine* and the *Normande*, a ship only a little larger, made it back into port. The two larger, but older, vessels sank with a loss of 200 Frenchmen. The *Dauphine* had to return to Dieppe.

Verrazano was discouraged, but yet another disappointment was awaiting him. King Francis had become involved in a dispute with Spain. The two countries were on the verge of declaring war. Verrazano was ordered to hand back the *Normande* to the king's service. What was he to do now? His two larger ships were on the bottom of the ocean, the *Normande* was reclaimed, and all he had

was the little *Dauphine*. Verrazano, how-ever, was not about to give up.

The *Dauphine* was a strongly built, three-masted vessel of less than 100 tons. She had been built originally for fishing in the treacherous seas off the New-foundland coast. Verrazano rerigged her with lateen (triangular) sails on two of her masts, instead of the usual square sails. From his experience in the Mediter-ranean, he regarded this type of sail as much more efficient and easily handled. Then he thoroughly repaired and over-hauled the vessel. Finally on January 2, 1524, the *Dauphine* put to sea with a crew of 50 men and enough provisions for eight months.

The expedition's financial backers were concerned that the Spanish would be furious if they found out that Ver-razano intended to sail to the new conti-nent by way of the Atlantic Ocean. So they told him to first sail south in order to back their story that they were sending him to the coast of North Africa on business. The coast bordered on the Mediterranean Sea and was easily reached from France. According to plan, Verrazano steered south and then slightly southwest to stop briefly at the uninhab-ited islet of Porto Santo, near Madeira. On January 17, he raised his anchor and headed west across the Atlantic.

Verrazano charted a course to land in the New World just north of the Spanish territory of Florida. With charts, com-pass, sea experience and lots of confi-dence, he sailed the *Dauphine* across the Atlantic, covering the 3,479 miles from Madeira in seven weeks. As the *Dauphine* drew near to the North American coast, a tremendous storm swept up from the south and drove the small ship north-ward for 36 hours.

Verrazano finally sighted land at a point only two degrees farther north than he had intended. The coast was that of present-day Wilmington, North Caro-lina. When the *Dauphine* came within a mile of land, the sailors could see that it was inhabited because huge fires had been built on the shore. The land stretched southward at this point and the

THE CONQUISTADORES — INVADERS OF THE NEW WORLD

Columbus should really be called the first "*conquistador*." After he returned from his initial trip in the New World with bits of gold gathered from the natives of Hispaniola, his find inspired a relentless search for more. The men who followed Columbus to the New World in search of gold and glory were known as the *conquistadores*, Spanish for "conquerors."

Most of the *conquistadores* were Spanish men who had fought in the wars of Europe, north Africa and Asia. They were bold and, in some cases, ruthless men. To them, the New World had free land and natives to work it.

Most of all, they believed that there was limitless gold and silver to make them rich. In their search for treasures, these Spanish soldiers conquered powerful Indian empires and mapped the lands of the new world.

Within twenty years of their discovery, nearly all the major islands of the Caribbean had been explored and several settlements established. The largest were on Hispaniola and Cuba. From there the *conquistadores* made their way onto the American mainland — to Panama, Mexico, Peru, Florida and the American Southwest, laying claim to all these lands for Spain.

Dauphine sailed along the coast in search of a good anchorage.

Verrazano continued down the coast for almost 200 miles without locating a passage through the continent. He had now gone about as far south as he dared. The Spanish would be very upset if they sighted him anywhere near Florida, to which they had made a very strong claim. So he turned north to search for the passage to the Indies.

Verrazano kept a log of his voyage, and up to this point his notes were very straightforward. But it appears that his mood began to change and he revealed another side of himself. His reports showed a great deal of sensitivity to the beauty and natural wonders of this new land. He took an interest in the native people and found that he could easily make friends with them.

On the voyage north, Verrazano made his first landing north of Cape Fear, the southernmost of North Carolina's three capes — Fear, Lookout, Hatteras — that extend like fingers into the sea. He saw many natives on the beach, but they fled when the *Dauphine* sailed closer. Several times they stopped and turned around to look at the ship in wonder. As the first to wade ashore, Verrazano approached the natives with his hands open in a show of friendship. They crowded around him and stared at his bearded face, his floppy hat, his elaborate clothing and the silver decorations on his sword.

The Indians were completely naked except for animal skins worn about their waists, and belts of grass, from which animal tails were hung. They were dark-skinned and their black hair was tied behind their heads like a tail. Verrazano described them as a little taller than the Frenchmen, with strong arms and well-formed bodies. They were very friendly and seemed to be sharp-witted and had great agility. Verrazano could see that they were also great runners. He compared them to people in certain parts of China.

The Frenchmen were so interested in the natives that they forgot to fill their water casks. Upon leaving, Verrazano set sail in a northeasterly direction, following the land. But by March 25 their drinking water was almost gone, so they had to anchor off the coast again to search for a source. Verrazano sent 25 men in a longboat to the shore. The surf was so rough that they were unable to make a landing. Many Indians came running to the beach to stare in wonder at the white Frenchmen and to wave to them.

Hoping to trade with the natives for water, Verrazano sent a strong swimmer through the surf with a bag of mirrors, bells and other trinkets. The sailor reached the shore and threw the goods onto the beach. But when he tried to return to the ship, the water was rougher than he had expected and he was tossed about mercilessly by the waves and hurled back up on the beach.

Verrazano watched in horror as the young sailor lay there half-dead. The natives then dragged him by the arms to a great fire on the beach. The sailor, realizing that he was being carried away, was stricken with terror and began to cry out. The Indians then started to remove his clothes.

At first, Verrazano and his crew thought that the natives were preparing to roast and eat the young sailor. But it turned out that they were just in wonder over his white body and had only meant to dry him out. When the sailor regained his strength, he showed them by signs that he wanted to return to his ship. With great kindness and affection, many of the Indians hugged him and accompanied him into the water. Then they retreated to a hill and stood watching until he was safe in the *Dauphine*.

Proceeding northwest, Verrazano followed a strip of land about a mile in width and 200 miles long. From the *Dauphine* he could see a great body of water on the other side of the narrow

PONCE de LEÓN

Ponce de León was a Spanish adventurer who sailed with Christopher Columbus on his second voyage in 1493 to the New World. There Ponce de León took part in the conquest of Hispaniola. He established the first Spanish settlement in Puerto Rico and in 1509 became its governor.

While serving as governor, Ponce de León learned of an island the Indians called Bimini, where there was supposedly a "fountain of youth" — a magic spring that would restore youth to the aged. In 1513, he set out to find Bimini and this magical fountain.

He landed near present-day Saint Augustine, Florida, and because of the many flowers he found there, he named the new land *Pascua Florida*, Spanish for "flowery Easter." The natives were very hostile, and he moved on to search for the fountain of youth. He sailed past Miami Bay and the Florida Keys and back to Puerto Rico, believing that the land he discovered was merely an island. He never did find Bimini, nor the fountain of youth. Other explorers proved Florida was not an island, but part of a big continent. Eventually the Spanish slaughtered most of the natives in Florida and it became part of the Spanish colonial empire.

strip. Verrazano thought this was the Pacific Ocean — the sea that borders on the shores of China. As they sailed along the coastline, the sailors strained their eyes to find a passage to the other side. But to Verrazano's disappointment, they found none.

What he had discovered was the Carolina Outer Banks, between Cape Lookout and north of Cape Hatteras. It is an isthmus, which is a strip of land that connects two larger land areas. The great body of water was Pamlico Sound. By assuming that he had found the Pacific Ocean, Verrazano made a tremendous geographical error. In fact, for over a century some maps and globes showed the Pacific Ocean flowing over forty percent of the future United States!

With his hopes high, Verrazano continued to search for a strait and a place to make a landing. Sailing along a beautiful green coast that was forested with tall trees, Verrazano sighted a small cove where they could anchor. They were now on the coast near what would become the Virginia–North Carolina border. Verrazano named the place Acadia, referring to a book by the same name, which describes an ancient wooded land of uncommon beauty. Of all the names given to areas along the coast by Verrazano, this is one of the few to survive. However, over the years, mapmakers gradually moved the name to the north and eastward. Finally an area covering part of

Nova Scotia, New Brunswick and Maine became known as Acadia.

At Acadia, Verrazano went ashore with 20 men. Awaiting them was an Indian man who seemed ready to take flight. Verrazano coaxed him to come near. The Indian, a handsome man with olive-colored skin and hair tied back in a knot, approached and held out a burning stick, as if to offer them fire. Verrazano thought his intention was hostile and ordered one of his men to fire his musket. The Indian trembled with fear. He fell to his knees and, pointing with his finger to the sky and then to the sea and the ship, he began to treat them as gods. The Indian had merely been offering a lit tobacco pipe as a sign of hospitality. Of course, the Frenchmen knew nothing about this custom and would not adopt

the tobacco habit until much later.

It was usual for explorers of this time to bring back natives to display before their king. Most natives would not come willingly, so they had to be taken by force. Verrazano was no different. He kidnapped a little boy to take back to France. In his log he recorded that he would have taken the mother, too, but she cried so loudly that they left her behind. Today this sort of behavior would be considered terribly cruel, but to Europeans of the time the natives of the New World were viewed more like animals than humans.

As Verrazano continued to sail northward, he missed the entrance to what would become the Chesapeake Bay. Had he seen it, he would have surely explored it as a passage to China. He sailed on-

ward, passing the shores of what would become Maryland, Delaware and New Jersey.

Then Verrazano spotted a place between two small but prominent hills. Between them was a wide, deep channel that flowed into the sea. Perhaps this was the passage to China. Verrazano anchored the *Dauphine* in the channel. He and his men rowed a small boat through what is now known as the "Narrows" between Staten Island and Long Island. Here they were met by as many as 30 canoes filled with Indians, who showed the Frenchmen a safe place to beach their boat. It was April 17, 1524.

The Indians were taller than the Frenchmen, of a bronze color with long, black hair, which they decorated. They wore lynx skins on their arms and deer skins around their loins. Some were dressed in bird feathers of many colors. Verrazano observed that they lived in cleverly built round huts and used straw mats to protect them from wind and rain. The women were beautiful and the Indian men showed great respect for them. This impressed Verrazano very much. He admired the fine workmanship of their marble-tipped arrows.

Here Verrazano saw a beautiful body of water about ten miles in circumference. This would become known as the

Upper Bay of Manhattan. Ahead he could see a river, which later became known as the Hudson River. Verrazano decided this was not the passage through the land. He would have liked to stay in this region with its friendly Indians, but a sudden, violent wind blew in from the sea. Doing what any good seaman would, Verrazano left with his men to make sure that the *Dauphine's* anchor cable was holding and that the ship was in no danger of drifting ashore.

As a compliment to King Francis I, Verrazano called the land and bay "Angoulême." (One of the King's titles was Count of Angoulême.) Once in his cabin, Verrazano wrote about the impressive bay, which he considered to be one of the finest harbors in the world. It was deep and wide enough for even the largest ships. How astonished Verrazano would have been to see, four centuries later, giant ocean liners docking in the same harbor below the skyscrapers of New York City.

Verrazano weighed anchor and sailed east along what is now Long Island and past Block Island. He was still certain that there was a passage through the new land. He wrote, "My intention was to reach Cathay [China] and I had not expected to find such an obstacle of new land. I thought it to be not without some strait to penetrate to the Eastern Ocean [the Pacific]."

The *Dauphine* next anchored in a beautiful bay later known as Narragansett Bay, off the coast of the future Newport, Rhode Island. The Indians here were the Wampanoag. They were so friendly and so curious about the white men that the Frenchmen stayed for two weeks.

Resuming her voyage eastward, for the land ran that way, the *Dauphine* passed Martha's Vineyard and Nantucket. She then rounded a prominent cape — now Cape Cod, Massachusetts. Still looking for a strait, Verrazano reached the coast of Maine near Casco Bay. Here he met the Abnaki Indians, who were not very friendly. Verrazano thought they were crude and, try as he could, he could not communicate with them. When he and his men went ashore, the Indians uttered loud war-cries, shot arrows at them and then fled into the woods. Verrazano called the coast of present-day Maine the "Land of Bad People." Of course, it is possible that the Indians thought that the strange white men were up to no good and merely wanted to chase them away.

Continuing along the coast of Maine, the *Dauphine* passed many inlets and some 32 islands. Verrazano thought that many of them would make good harbors. He also admired the rare beauty of the region — the turquoise sea flashing in the sunlight and the magnificent rocky coast.

The *Dauphine* then approached Newfoundland, the land discovered by John Cabot in 1497. From there, Verrazano set out across the Atlantic toward France. With favorable winds, he reached Dieppe on July 8, 1524. The *Dauphine*'s voyage had lasted a little over six months.

Once again an explorer had set out to find a particular place and had come across another that was totally unexpected. Verrazano had failed to discover a passage to China. And by mistaking Pamlico Sound for the Pacific Ocean, he added to Europe's confusion concerning the New World. However, he had discovered 2,000 miles of unknown coastline, proving that there was an unbroken continent between South Carolina and Newfoundland, not islands, as had been supposed.

But what lay beyond the coast — one continent or several? That important question still had to be answered. Verrazano had not found a northern strait, and he was fairly sure that none existed. He now believed that a passage westward across the continent lay in some undiscovered place in the Caribbean Sea (that is, Central America).

Verrazano's Florentine and French investors were disappointed with the results of the voyage. Coastlines and Indians did not interest them nearly as much as a quick sea route to the Far East. They decided not to finance another expedition.

King Francis, however, encouraged Verrazano to pursue his new idea of a route from the Caribbean Sea. He introduced him to Philippe de Chabot, admiral of the French navy, who became Verrazano's patron and advisor.

With the French merchants no longer able to pay the high prices for imported silk and spices, Philippe de Chabot knew that France had to establish its own trade route with the Indies. But he knew the French could not use Portugal's sea route around southern Africa because that country would be swift to resent their presence there. And he was afraid to let Verrazano find a shorter and quicker route by way of the Caribbean, if it existed, because this was Spanish territory.

Chabot decided to use Magellan's newly discovered strait as the way to the Spice Islands. It was safer because Spain had no settlements that far south and the French would not be trespassing on their possessions in the New World.

It was 1527 and Verrazano was now

about 46 years old. His hair and beard were turning gray, but he still had the burning desire for exploration of his younger days. In June, he set out with three ships, sailing across the Atlantic Ocean to the mouth of the Amazon River (in northern Brazil) and southward toward Magellan's strait. His brother, Gierolamo, accompanied him this time, curious to see the countries and coastlines he charted on maps.

Heavy gales kept Verrazano and his little fleet from passing through the strait, a dangerous sailing feat even in the best of weather. So he ordered his ships to turn about and steer across the Atlantic to the Cape of Good Hope. If he could not reach the Spice Islands by the westerly route, then he would try the easterly route across the Indian Ocean.

By the winter of 1527, the fleet had reached the Cape of Good Hope. Easterly gales and 50-foot waves battered the vessels. After several weeks of battling the sea, one of the ships managed to pass eastward into the Indian Ocean. Verrazano's own ship and the one carrying his brother were unable to follow.

Verrazano decided to give up the struggle because his ships could not continue to fight the pounding. But he was determined not to go back to France empty-handed this time. So he sailed westward again, this time to the northern coast of Brazil to load up with brazilwood, which produced a valuable scarlet dye. The weary seamen cut and loaded the timber and then sailed back to France. Verrazano arrived in France on September 15, 1527, after a voyage lasting 15 months and covering a total distance of 20,000 miles.

The Florentine bankers and merchants were highly impressed with Verrazano's navigational feat and the profits from the brazilwood. They offered to finance a third voyage to seek a passage that was supposedly located in the land to the west of Cuba (that is, the upper part of South America).

At the age of 48 or so, Verrazano began his last voyage in April, 1528. With several ships, all merchant vessels chartered for the voyage, he set his course toward Florida. Florentine and French authorities were very quiet about the expedition. They did not want any word to leak out about Verrazano's destination. If the Spanish found out, they would surely try to stop the expedition.

Soon after sighting and steering clear of the Florida peninsula, Verrazano's ships passed on to the Bahamian Islands. They stopped only briefly to gather fresh fruit and water. Next Verrazano led the fleet southward past Puerto Rico to Trin-

idad. Then the ships turned west and began to cruise along the green coast of what is now Venezuela (at the top of the South American continent).

The crews complained that Verrazano seemed to be in a great hurry and was giving them no time to anchor for a night or two of rest. He was direct with them: "A night spent in harbor is half a day and a whole tide wasted, and it may mean an advance of 40 miles thrown away. The more days we spend in the sea, the more likely the Spanish are to learn of our presence here." So the ships sailed without a break until they reached the Gulf of Darien on the northwest coast of South America.

There Verrazano set off in a longboat with six of his crew to search for fruit and fresh water. A small band of natives waited near the shore. Verrazano walked up the white, pebbly beach with his hands outstretched in friendship. He did not know that these natives were hostile because white men had invaded their land 20 years earlier.

As he approached within a few yards, the natives stooped to grab weapons they had hidden in the undergrowth at their feet. When they stood up again, they launched poisoned arrows and short, barbed spears at the white men. Verrazano and his men fell dead on the beach.

Fearing the loss of more lives, Gierolamo and the other captains decided against sending a landing party to attack the murderers in the dense jungle. Shocked and saddened by the loss of their leader, the French sailed out of the Caribbean Sea. The fleet stopped on the coast of Brazil to load their holds with cargoes of dye-wood and then sailed home to France. The ships reached Dieppe in March, 1529.

Giovanni da Verrazano's death was greatly mourned throughout France and Italy. However, his lack of success in finding a strait caused other explorers to look for one farther north.

Over 400 years later, Verrazano's first voyage, in 1524, along the coast of a vast continent that he had not expected to find, is considered to be one of the greatest events in the history of North American discovery. His account is of tremendous historical value even today, for it provided the earliest description of the country and the Indian tribes along the Atlantic coast north of Florida.

It was not until the 1900s that Verrazano was acknowledged as the explorer who discovered New York Harbor. In 1964, when a bridge connecting Staten Island and Brooklyn was erected between the Lower and Upper Bay, it bore the name of Verrazano.

JACQUES CARTIER

Jacques Cartier was born in 1491 in Saint-Malo, an island off the north coast of France. He grew up surrounded by the wild North Atlantic sea. The tides sometimes rose as high as 50 feet and hurled waves against the granite walls that protected the town. Tides like these taught the young Jacques how to use his wits in handling small boats.

His father was a fisherman. As a young boy, Jacques learned how to sail and fish while accompanying him on fishing trips in the North Atlantic.

In 1497, when Jacques Cartier was still a small boy in Saint-Malo, John Cabot set out from England to find a quick route to Asia. This much sought-after route became known as the "Northwest Passage." Cabot never found it, but he did find the icy, mountainous land of Newfoundland (now part of Canada). His discovery did not interest most Europeans because he did not bring home any gold or treasures. But the people of Saint-Malo were interested because Cabot said that the shallow water off the coast of Newfoundland was abundant with codfish and halibut. So each spring the merchants of Saint-Malo sent fleets to the fishing grounds, which became known as the Grand Banks.

Jacques Cartier went with his father on many trips across the Atlantic to the Grand Banks. He saw the east coast of Newfoundland with its high snow-covered mountains in the distance and often wondered what lay beyond. But none of the other fishermen seemed curious. Every spring Jacques left for the Grand Banks and every autumn he returned disappointed that they never explored any farther than the fishing grounds.

By the time he was 30 years old, Jacques Cartier had become captain of his own fishing boat. Unfortunately, the fishermen he hired were afraid to sail any farther than the Grand Banks because they imagined all kinds of dangers lurking in the unknown. And Jacques did not make enough money to pay for an expedition himself.

Cartier decided that he must find wealth in some other way. Tired of the North Atlantic's harsh weather and the hard work of fishing, he took a job as the captain of a Portuguese trading vessel bound for the shores of Brazil (on the northeast coast of South America). He had heard that the natives there would trade gold for simple things like fishhooks and mirrors. But Cartier was unlucky. By the time he reached Brazil, the natives had already sold much of their gold to other European seamen.

Cartier was very disappointed, but when he returned to the beat of the sea against the walls of Saint-Malo, he realized how much he loved the wild North Atlantic. Somehow, he would find a way to sail beyond the Grand Banks.

He now had a reputation among seamen as one of the best captains in France. Philippe de Chabot, admiral of the French navy, heard of Jacques Cartier's expert navigational skills. He, too, was very interested in finding the Northwest Passage and asked Cartier to attempt to find it. Cartier said yes, but he told the admiral that he was also interested in exploring the land that blocked the way between Europe and China (that is, North America). The admiral told Cartier to first find the waterway from the Atlantic Ocean to the Pacific Ocean;

then bring back a full report on everything he saw. Chabot told him that France would pay for everything. For Cartier, it was the dream of a lifetime come true.

He chose two small vessels, each weighing 60 tons. They would be fast and easy to maneuver. Then he hired 60 French fishermen for each ship and took on enough provisions to last from April until early fall. On the morning of April 20, 1534, Jacques Cartier, at the age of 42, sailed out of the harbor of Saint-Malo.

In 20 days the wind blew his ships across two thousand miles of ocean and he saw the mountains of Newfoundland rising above the horizon. The stiff east winds that had swept Cartier so rapidly across the Atlantic had also driven masses of Arctic ice against the Newfoundland coast. The two little ships took shelter in a harbor, where they waited ten days for the winds to change and the ice to clear. Then they sailed toward the northern tip of Newfoundland.

Cartier now sailed along the border between the known and the unknown. But the French fishermen had never gone beyond the Grand Banks, and their fears began to grow. In the mist, fog and ice-filled seas, they still believed there were sea monsters. Although the sailors did not see any, they did come across many strange creatures.

The two ships finally came upon an island that Cartier called the "Isle of Birds" because of the huge number of sea birds that covered the rocks and hovered above it. The sailors rowed their boats through the ice to the island, where they caught large black-and-white birds as big as geese. They were easy to catch because they could not fly. These were great auks, which eventually became extinct because humans found them so easy to kill for food. But there were other birds, the gannets, that fought back and "bit like dogs."

The sailors saw another animal that was as big as a cow, as white as a swan and could swim as fast as they could row their boats through the water. It was a polar bear that had swum out to the island to catch birds. The sailors killed it and enjoyed their first taste of bear meat.

Cartier continued north along the northern tip of Newfoundland. There was a channel stretching westward, which he thought was the mouth of a great passage leading to China. He steered into the opening, which later became known as the Strait of Belle Isle. It was not the Northwest Passage, but the strait that separates Newfoundland from the coast of Labrador (both are provinces

of Canada today). It was still spring when Cartier turned west and entered the strait. They saw gigantic icebergs that had broken away from glaciers and were drifting through the waterway to the ocean. The icebergs were beautiful to look at, but dreaded by the sailors.

Cartier picked his way carefully through the floating islands of ice. Suddenly a small birchbark canoe appeared in the mist ahead. Two young Indians stared up in awe and terror at the monsters of wood and canvas gliding toward them. The French seamen gazed down curiously at the brown-skinned natives. The Indians seemed relieved to see men looking down at them. They must have thought that gods or monsters were in the strange craft. Responding to Cartier's signs to climb aboard, they were given biscuits and meat. The Indians wore nothing above the waist and the cold weather did not seem to bother them. Their heads were shaved, except for a few locks on top. Using sign language, they told the Frenchmen that they were on a fishing trip and had come from somewhere to the west. As the ship sailed through the strait, they were content to stay on board, eating and trying on the sailors' caps and shirts.

In June, Cartier headed south along the west coast of Newfoundland, which has a length of about 300 miles. He was now sailing on a vast, uncharted expanse of water that he believed to be a large bay. He had no way of knowing that he was on the gulf of one of the world's greatest rivers, the Saint Lawrence. Sailing down this "Great Bay," as he called it, he had to fight heavy mists and fog. Cartier had only crude navigational instruments, but like all great navigators, he also had an instinct that took the place of scientific equipment.

On the 24th of June, the two ships reached Newfoundland's headland, now called Cape Anguille. Cartier had no idea where he was, but decided to turn southwest to search for the passage to China. Summer had arrived and the Frenchmen discovered many islands covered with lush green shrubs and trees. They were quite happy to have left the bleak, gray coasts of Newfoundland. Cartier named one of the islands Brion after Philippe de Chabot, one of whose titles was Seigneur de Brion. It reminded him very much of France, with fields of flowers, gooseberry bushes, strawberry plants, roses and other fragrant herbs. The abundance of spices made Cartier think that China could not be far away.

On Brion Island the sailors saw bears, foxes and other animals known to them. There were also strange creatures that Cartier described in his log as large, clumsy oxen with two tusks like those of an elephant. Two sailors tried to capture one of the strange beasts while it slept on the shore. But when the men came close, the massive beast awoke and escaped to the water. It was a walrus.

The ships continued to sail southwest and dropped anchor on what is today called the North Point of Prince Edward Island. Cartier gave this headland the name Cape Savage because of a lone Indian who beckoned from the shore. But when a boat was put over the side and some sailors began to row toward him, he grew alarmed and fled. But the sailors left behind a trinket before rowing back to the ship. Cartier did not record what was given to the Indian.

On July 4, 1534, Cartier reached a

headland (northern point of Miscou Island), which he named Cape Hope because to the north he could see miles and miles of shimmering water. He thought that he had found the route to China and steered his ships in that direction. But he soon discovered that it was not a passage at all, but a deep-water bay. Cartier called it Chaleur Bay, meaning Bay of Heat, because the air was so warm there. Today the waters of Chaleur Bay wash up on the shores of two Canadian provinces — Quebec and New Brunswick.

Cartier was now very curious about this land that lay between him and China. It had no European name and did not yet exist on any maps. Everywhere he looked was wilderness. He anchored his two ships in a cove within the bay and went in a longboat to explore the shores of what is the Gaspé Peninsula. The land was good for farming and there were wonderful forests full of cedars and spruce that would make good masts for ships. While Cartier explored in his long-boat, a party of 50 Indians canoed silently into the bay and surrounded him. Taken by surprise, he fired two shots over their heads. The Indians promptly retreated to the land, where they yelled and beckoned the Frenchmen to come ashore.

The next day, nine canoes filled with natives advanced toward the ships. Yelling and waving animal skins, they indicated that they wished to trade with the sailors. Cartier decided that they seemed friendly enough to risk going ashore. When the Frenchmen stepped out of their longboat, the curious natives touched their white skins and pulled gently at their beards. Hundreds of Indian men, squaws and children gathered to see the strangers.

The Frenchmen were just as curious about the bronze-skinned natives, who were members of the Micmac tribe on a fishing expedition. They wore their hair long and were naked except for the animal pelts worn about their waists and other pelts thrown over their shoulders. Cartier gave them knives, combs, beads and bells. Eager to receive more gifts, the Indians surrounded the white men, giving them furs and all they had on until they were practically naked.

But more valuable to Cartier than the furs were the two Micmac words he learned and entered in his logbook: *cochy*, which meant hatchet, and *becan*, which meant knife. If he could learn more of their language, he would be able to communicate with them better.

On July 12, Cartier left Chaleur Bay and the friendly natives to continue his search for the passage to China. He sailed east to beautiful Gaspé Bay and anchored there. It was not long before the Frenchmen were greeted by over two hundred Indians in 40 canoes. They were Hurons, also on a fishing expedition far from their home at a place called Kebec. Like the Micmac, they wore little clothing, except for loin cloths and furs over their shoulders. Their heads were shaved, leaving only top knots tied with leather thongs. Their chief was an elderly man named Donnacona, who seemed completely unafraid of the strange white men. Cartier easily made friends with the Hurons by giving them gifts of knives, combs and glass beads.

The Frenchmen felt confident enough to row ashore often to feast with the natives in their temporary camp. However, the Hurons' mood began to

He was too busy hatching a scheme to take two of the Indians back to France to show them to the king. That would allow Cartier to teach them French so they could interpret for him when he returned to this vast wilderness.

To distract the natives, Cartier held out an axe as a sign that he wanted to trade for furs. When the chief's two sons came closer in their canoe, sailors jumped aboard and dragged them back to Cartier's ship. The Frenchmen then dressed the two young men in shirts, coats and caps, and put copper chains around their necks. Cartier gave them food to show Donnacona that they would be treated well and indicated that they would be returned with many goods from France. The chief's sons, named Taignoagny and Domagaya, seemed pleased to be setting out on such a fine adventure. Donnacona, having little choice and believing that they would be treated well, agreed to let them go.

change when Cartier's men put up a 30-foot cross with the inscription, "Long live the King of France." The Indians guessed that the white men were claiming the land for themselves. And of course they were right. Cartier saw their displeasure and tried to convince them that the cross was just a marker to help him find his way back.

But Donnacona did not trust the white men. He paddled out to the ships with his two sons and several other men. The chief pointed to the cross and shook his head. Then he stretched out his hands to indicate that the land was the home of the Hurons. But Cartier was unmoved.

The ships sailed out of Gaspé Bay on July 25 into a rolling fog. They headed northeast and reached an island now named Anticosti (in the middle of the Gulf of Saint Lawrence). The ships worked their way westward along the north coast of Anticosti and reached a strait, which is now called Jacques Cartier Strait. The wind blew them back from the entrance, but Cartier could see an expanse of water beyond that stretched westward as far as the eye could see (this was the mouth of the great Saint Lawrence River). He thought that it was surely the passage to China and wanted to follow where it led.

But the days were growing shorter and the nights colder. Cartier knew that he had to leave this wilderness before the winds changed or else the winter ice would imprison his ships without enough supplies and food. The safety of his men came first. So he pointed his ships toward home, taking the two young Indians with him.

On September 5, Cartier docked in Saint-Malo and immediately went to see Chabot. Eager to return to the New World as soon as possible, he told the admiral that he had probably found the Northwest Passage. When King Francis heard the news, he was disappointed that Cartier had not found any gold or treasure. But the passage would open up the riches of the east for France, so he agreed to send Cartier on a second voyage.

This time Cartier asked for three larger ships and more men. After making his preparations, he left Saint-Malo on May 19, 1535. Cartier's largest ship, the *Grande Hermine*, was 120 tons, which was very large in those days. Next was the

Petite Hermine, 60 tons, and then the *Émerillon*, a 40-ton fishing vessel. Aboard the three ships were 112 French fishermen who had already made many voyages to the fishing grounds of Newfoundland. Among them were the two Indians, who after nine months in Saint-Malo had learned to speak and understand the French language fairly well. They would be valuable as guides and interpreters.

This time Cartier led his expedition through Belle Isle Strait and across the northern section of the "Great Bay" (now called the Gulf of Saint Lawrence) toward Anticosti Island. It was a dangerous route because there were thousands of islands and many shoals and hidden rocks along the coast of Labrador. Cartier stopped frequently to take soundings by lowering a rope into the water to measure the depth. He recorded this in his logbook, together with other information of interest to navigators, since he was sure this would become a much-used route to China.

In early August, Cartier reached the rocky, black shores of Anticosti Island and the beginning of the waterway to the west. Heavy storms in the channel between the island and the mainland prevented him from entering the passage. So the three ships anchored at a bay on the mainland. It happened to be the feast day of Saint Lawrence and Cartier named the bay in honor of him.

As soon as the winds stopped, the three ships headed westward on their course. With flags flying, they passed the northwest tip of Anticosti and entered the waterway. Cartier could tell from its salty water and regular tides that it was a sea route. At last he had found the Northwest Passage to China! Or so he thought.

Taignoagny and Domagaya pointed excitedly to the land, saying that they were nearing their home. They told Cartier that if he sailed up the waterway they would come to "kannata," which meant settlement. The word was later changed to "Canada" and used to refer to the land mass that Cartier discovered. The natives' village was called Stadacona. They told him that farther up the waterway the channel grew narrower and the water became fresh. The waterway was so long that they had never heard of anyone reaching its source. With this news, Cartier's face became grim. Now he realized that this was not a passage to China, but a river.

Deeply disappointed, he spent a few days exploring the mouth of the river, which he found to be 80 miles wide! He realized then that the "Great Bay" was not a bay at all, but the gulf of a mighty river. Soon the discovery began to absorb his attention. The Indians called it the River of Hochelaga. Cartier called it the Great River of Canada (kannata). In later years it was named the Saint Lawrence River. Cartier decided to sail up the waterway, hoping that the passage to China lay in the lands of the north.

Cartier headed westward. He was such a skillful navigator that he managed to avoid all the shoals and treacherous eddies that could wreck a ship. Soon the river began to work its magic on him. He forgot all about his disappointment and was filled with the joy of seeing curiosities and wonders for the first time. Nature itself was the spectacle.

Here was a vast wilderness, abundant with wildlife. The Frenchmen saw elk, deer and moose. In the waters were salmon, eels and lampreys, plus strange creatures that Cartier described as very large fish, as white as snow and without a spot. They lacked fins and had a body and head like a greyhound. There were many of them living in the river between the salt and fresh water. The Indians called them "*adothuys*" and said they were good to eat. What Cartier described in his log were beluga whales.

As they sailed up the Saint Lawrence, Taignoagny and Domagaya told Cartier about the land through which the ships

FRENCH EXPLORERS

In 1608 Samuel de Champlain founded a settlement near Stadacona that grew into the city of Quebec. He also explored Lake Ontario and Lake Huron. Étienne Brulé discovered the world's largest fresh-water lake, Lake Superior. And Father Jacques Marquette and Louis Joliet explored the Mississippi River region south of the Great Lakes. Their work was followed up by René-Robert La Salle, who made a journey down the Mississippi River to the Gulf of Mexico.

were passing. On the north side of the great waterway lay a number of tribal lands. Many canoe trips up the river was the kingdom of Hochelaga, the Indian word for "beaver dam," or "place where the river is obstructed." The inhabitants of these kingdoms were the Huron.

Five hundred miles from Anticosti Island, Cartier approached the tribal lands of Taignoagny and Domagaya. The river was a lot narrower here and the ships anchored in a quiet channel between high, gray cliffs and a little island that Cartier named the Isle of Orleans. Taignoagny and Domagaya saw some of their tribesmen fishing nearby. "We call this area Kebec," they told Cartier. (The word "kebec" means "narrow." It is now spelled "Quebec," and is the name of a province of Canada.) As Cartier ad-

vanced his ships a little farther up the river, the people in the Indian town of Stadacona saw them approach. The two natives on board waved. When they had last seen their friends and relatives, they were off the Gaspé Peninsula on a fishing expedition.

On September 8, Donnacona came aboard and greeted Cartier, happy to see his sons back home. After a big feast with the Hurons, Cartier set out in the ships' boats to explore upstream and find a good harbor for his ships. He found it at the junction of the Saint Lawrence and the Saint Charles Rivers, where the village of Stadacona was located. When he anchored his ships, the men, women and children came out to greet the French mariners and the two men they had given up for lost. The braves had decorated their bare brown bodies with stripes of blue, red and white clay. Their long black hair was ornamented with bright feathers. Clusters of wampum and beads made from seashells dangled from leather straps around their necks.

Donnacona, his two sons and others of the chief's council boarded Cartier's ship for a meeting. Cartier asked Donncona about the "great river" and the kingdom of Hochelaga. But the Indians tried to talk him out of further exploration of the river. Donnacona told

Cartier of rapids, whirlpools, sudden gales and evil spirits lurking in the forests. But Cartier was determined to explore farther up the river and perhaps even find the Northwest Passage. Donnacona saw Cartier's determination and thought up an elaborate scheme to frighten him.

Later, while the Frenchmen were all aboard their ships, a canoe came drifting toward them. In it were three fiendish-looking creatures wrapped in white-and-black dogs' skins. Their faces were as black as coal and long horns rose from their foreheads. This was the queerest sight Cartier had yet seen in Canada. From a distance, the creatures looked like devils. But as they came nearer, it was obvious that they were Indians in elaborate costumes. They stood up in the canoe when they passed the ships and shouted loudly at Cartier. Then they drifted to shore, where for a half hour a loud powwow could be heard.

The next day, Taignoagny and Domagaya told Cartier that the devils he saw were messengers from God sent to tell them that there would be ice and cold in Hochelaga. Cartier tried not to laugh. He knew that Donnacona was trying to scare him, but he did not know why. Later Cartier discovered that the chief of Hochelaga was a Huron who claimed to be Stadacona's ruler. Donnacona obvi-ously thought that with the French as his friends, with their ships, firearms and iron tools, he could defeat his rival. But Cartier did not want to get involved in the politics of the Indian nations and he decided to explore farther.

On September 19, 1535, Cartier and 50 of his men set sail for Hochelaga. He left the two larger ships and a crew in Kebec to build a fort and prepare for winter. It was fall. The hardwood trees were ablaze in colors of gold and scarlet — oaks, elms, spruce, ash, willows. The great forests were filled with cranes, geese, ducks, pheasants, blackbirds and many other kinds of birds. Cartier watched and listened in wonder, record-ing his impressions in his log book.

After nine days, the Frenchmen found that the river widened so much that it looked like a lake. Upon reaching a cluster of islands, Cartier launched two longboats and took 28 men to explore farther. After discovering a passage be-tween the islands, the Frenchmen rowed on for three more days, until they saw a mountain on an island in the middle of the river. On the shore below was the huge Indian town of Hochelaga. The date was October 2, 1535.

The settlement was built in a great circle surrounded by three rows of high walls made of tree trunks. Over 50 wooden long-houses covered with bark stood inside the walls. More than one thousand people stood at the river's edge to greet them. When Cartier came ashore, they crowded around him and his men. The Indians marveled at the Frenchmen and pressed in close to touch their clothing and beards.

For five days, the Frenchmen feasted with the natives. They were entertained by dancing around great bonfires in the center of the village. Cartier observed a strange custom. The Indians filled one end of a hollow piece of wood with dried leaves, which they lit with a hot coal. Then they sucked on the other end of the tube, filling their lungs with smoke and letting it come out their mouths and noses. Cartier tried it, but the smoke burned his mouth. It would be a number of years before Europeans would make tobacco a part of their lives.

One morning, believing Cartier was a god, the Indians brought their lame, blind and crippled to him to be cured. Cartier did not know what to do. He was not a doctor and certainly not a god. The only thing he could think to do was to say prayers for them. So he stood up, stretched out one hand and prayed aloud in a deep, solemn voice. The Indians stood in wonder, but it is doubtful that any were cured.

Before leaving Hochelaga, Cartier wanted to get a bird's-eye view of the region that lay beyond. Guides led him and his men to the mountain in the middle of the island. Cartier called it Mont Réal, meaning "royal mountain." (Later these two words were combined to make the word Montréal. It is now a major city in Quebec.) When he reached the top, Cartier could see the great river flowing speedily over three miles of rocky rapids where the current swirled and boiled. No ship could pass through that part of the river, even though it might lead to China. Through sign language, he learned that there were more rapids ahead and that other rivers fed into the Great River. He wanted to explore them, but for now he had to return to Kebec.

On October 11, 1535, Cartier arrived

at his winter quarters in Kebec on the banks of the Saint Charles River. The men he had left behind had built a strong wooden fort. The walls had been made by driving logs upright into the earth. Inside the fortress, the sailors had built a number of huts from heavy timber and had installed iron stoves brought from the ships. The ships had been towed into the mouth of the river close to the fort so the crews could keep watch on them during the winter.

November arrived and brought the cold northern weather with it. Then in December the Frenchmen experienced their first blizzard. While snow rose against the walls of the fort, they huddled around their hot stoves. Indians came daily to visit and the sailors were amazed at their ability to walk waist-deep through the snow wearing little clothing but their leggings and moccasins.

Donnacona and Cartier spent many hours talking. The chieftain told Cartier of the riches of a tribal kingdom called Saguenay, where the people dressed in fine clothes. He said that the fastest and safest route was the River of Hochelaga to a place where it was joined by another river (the Ottawa) that flowed down from the kingdom of Saguenay. From the mouth of the Ottawa, the journey would take one month. Cartier was very interested in exploring the kingdom of Saguenay because he thought it must be a part of China. The more he could find out from Donnacona, the better. But then the talks suddenly came to an end.

The Indians did not come to the fort anymore. It turned out that many had come down with a disease. On top of that, Taignoagny warned Cartier that the warriors of Stadacona were talking of raiding the Frenchmen's camp to obtain knives, blankets, axes, nails and fishing lines.

At the end of December, the Frenchmen came down with the same disease. It was scurvy, caused by lack of fresh fruit and vegetables. The sailors' arms and legs swelled, their teeth loosened and fell out and their bodies became covered with sores.

By the end of January, 1536, twenty-five men were dead. Only Cartier and three others remained in good health. It was up to them to keep a constant watch for hostile Indians. The rest of the men were too weak from scurvy to even stand up. Indians began to lurk about the fort. Cartier feared if they learned how weak his crew had grown, they might attack. So whenever the Indian warriors approached, Cartier ordered his men to hammer loudly with sticks on the floor and walls. He told them to sing and shout and laugh, pretending they were all working hard and were in good spirits. The trick seemed to work. For every time the Indians came, they paused and listened for a while and then went away.

One day Domagaya approached the fort. Cartier went out to meet him. He said that one of his men was sick with the disease and asked him how his people recovered so quickly. Domagaya told Cartier about a brew they made from the leaves of a certain tree. Cartier asked if one of these trees was nearby. Domagaya pointed to an evergreen and told Cartier to strip off the bark and foliage, boil it for several hours and drink the water while it was still warm.

Cartier immediately found an axe and chopped off branches and bark. He and the other three men boiled the needles and bark as quickly as they could and gave the brew to the sick sailors. Within six days, after consuming practically the whole tree, the men were all strong and healthy again. It seemed like a miracle, but it was really the vitamin C in the evergreen tree.

By the end of March, the snow was melting and the ice on the river started to break apart. Cartier knew that it was time to return home. Nearly a year had passed since he had sailed from France. Yet he had not found the Northwest Passage.

And even if the Great River led to China, how could ships pass the rapids near Hochelaga? All Cartier had discovered was a river and a wilderness. What would he tell the king?

Cartier thought about the mighty river he had discovered. It teemed with fish, enriched the soil of the land and sustained the mighty forests. The land had enough wildlife to feed many more people than the Indian tribes. The idea to set up a French colony in this vast wilderness seemed natural to him. Cartier began to dream of the day when the land would be filled with farms, towns and water mills.

But he knew it would be difficult to convince the king of such a plan. Cartier had not found any gold, silver or other treasures, as the Spanish had done in the southern lands. Then he remembered that Donnacona had spoken of the distant kingdom of Saguenay, where such treasures supposedly could be found. But surely the French king would not believe him. At this point, Cartier decided that Donnacona must go back to France with him to tell the king about Saguenay. But surely Donnacona would not go willingly!

Once again, Cartier planned a kidnapping. When Donnacona came to visit with ten of his friends, the Frenchmen seized them and hurried them aboard the ships. On May 6, 1536, while Indians stood on the shore wailing for their chief, the anchors were raised, sails were set, and the vessels departed for France. Donnacona accepted his fate and was encouraged by Cartier's promise to return him in a year with gifts for his people.

This time Cartier wanted to find a shorter route home, so he entered the Gulf through the southern arm of the Great River between Anticosti and the Gaspé Peninsula. The new route was not difficult and Cartier continued to navigate southeastward until he discovered a strait (now known as the Cabot Strait, passing between the provinces of Nova Scotia and Newfoundland). He was very pleased when the passage led him quickly to the Atlantic. Good winds and favorable seas permitted him to reach Saint-Malo on July 15, 1536.

France and Spain were at war when Cartier reached home. The king was too busy to think about Canada, Indian chiefs and voyages of exploration. Even Chabot could not help him because he had fallen out of favor with the king. Cartier had to go back to deep-sea fishing. And the kidnapped Indians, not used to European diseases, rich food and living indoors, died one by one, until none were left.

Five years passed before anyone became interested in Cartier's plan for establishing a colony in Canada. Count François de Roberval, a wealthy businessman, was attracted by the treasures and the furs that Cartier said were abundant in the new land. Although Cartier did not trust him, he knew that Roberval had the power and the money to arrange another voyage.

Because money was greatly needed to fill the coffers of the French treasury, Roberval was able to persuade King Francis to back another voyage. Cartier was given five ships this time, but unfortunately no one would volunteer to settle in the wilderness. Therefore the colonists were recruited from prisons: murderers, thieves and criminals of all kinds. They

chose to stay behind. Cartier feared that if he told the truth, the Indians would not believe that their friends had simply died. They would surely think that they had been murdered.

The Indians paddled back to shore in silence. This time there was no invitation to join them in a feast. Cartier knew that they would never trust him again. Not taking any chances, he sailed 12 miles upstream and anchored off the mouth of a river later named Cap Rouge. Here Cartier set up the first French colony and named it Charlesbourg-Royal.

To Cartier's surprise, on the shore of the Cap Rouge River, he found nuggets that he believed to be gold. And on the slopes of a neighboring mountain, he found crystal-like stones that appeared to be diamonds. The kingdom of Saguenay with its riches seemed more attainable than before.

Cartier immediately planned a trip to the rapids of Mont Réal so that in the following spring he might lead an expedition over the rapids to the mouth of the Ottawa River. But he would not begin until the settlement on the Cap Rouge River was established.

On September 7, 1541, Cartier set out with two longboats to survey the route to the kingdom of Saguenay. After he reached Hochelaga, he succeeded in

would not make the best pioneers, to say the least.

On May 23, 1541, Carter set sail on his third voyage to the Canadian wilderness. Count de Roberval was to follow with four ships carrying reinforcements of men and supplies. At the end of June, Cartier made his landfall in Canada. A few weeks later, the fleet drew near the familiar village of Stadacona. It had changed little in five years.

Canoes filled with Indians rushed out to meet the ships and welcome home their chieftain. When they did not see Donnacona, they asked Cartier where he was. Seeing their sullen faces, Cartier knew that he would have to pay for kidnapping their chief. He told them that Donnacona had died and that the other men had married French women and

passing through the first rapids, Saint Mary's Current, by double-manning one of his longboats. Then he proceeded with the single boat to the second barrier of rapids, the Lachine. However, he could not pass through because the current was too swift and the rocks were too treacherous.

Cartier and his men continued on foot along the river's bank. Finally they met some Indians and asked them how far it was to the kingdom of Saguenay and if it could be reached by water. The Indians said the trip to Saguenay would take many moons and was impossible to reach by water. This confused Cartier terribly. Now he had no idea where Saguenay or China was. All he was sure of was that he stood somewhere in a vast wilderness unknown to Europeans.

Cartier returned to his colony at Charlesbourg-Royal to find that his 200 criminal colonists were beginning to grow afraid of this strange, lonely country. Ice was forming on the water and would soon lock them in the wilderness for the winter. And Roberval had not shown up with reinforcements.

To add to his problems, the Indians did not trust Cartier anymore. Sometimes an arrow would streak out of the forest and bury its tip in the walls of the fort. This was the Indian way of showing that the white Frenchmen were no longer welcome in their land. Cartier ordered the fort to be strengthened and the colonists sat out the winter in fear.

When spring came at last, the Frenchmen were eager to leave this land of harsh winters and lurking enemies. Cartier knew that his colonists were close to mutiny and that he could no longer keep them in the wilderness. He would have to sail back to France without having reached the kingdom of Saguenay or finding the Northwest Passage. But he hoped that the nuggets of gold and the diamonds he had found would make up for his failure.

The ships sailed down the Saint Lawrence and headed toward home. Along the southwest coast of Newfoundland, Cartier sighted the white sails of Count de Roberval, who was finally coming to join him. The count ordered Cartier to accompany him to Charlesbourg-Royal. But Cartier refused, not wishing to see his men suffer hunger, fear, loneliness and death again in the vast wilderness. He continued eastward across the Atlantic to Saint-Malo, while Roberval's ships headed toward Canada.

Back in France, the "gold" and "diamonds" were tested. They proved to be worthless. The gold turned out to be iron pyrite, which later became known as

"fool's gold." And the diamonds were simply mica, a transparent mineral. As a result, a saying came into usage: "False as a diamond of Canada." The mockery and laughter that followed brought Cartier's career as an explorer to a quick end.

Roberval returned to France in 1543. He had failed miserably with both his colony and his attempts to find the riches of Saguenay. Canada was left to its original inhabitants, the Native Americans — at least for the time being.

Cartier spent the last years of his life quietly in Saint-Malo, where he could see and hear the Atlantic Ocean. Mapmakers and geographers consulted with him there. He died in 1557 at the age of 66 without receiving the public recognition due him. Unfortunately few people understood the value of his explorations.

Cartier's journeys had greatly increased Europeans' knowledge of North America. Lost in the vast wilderness of Canada, he had discovered the mighty Saint Lawrence River, a source of wealth more precious than gold mines. And, contrary to his expectations, he proved that the river was *not* the Northwest Passage to China.

Cartier's explorations sparked other Frenchmen to seek out the mysteries of Canada. Later many settlements sprang up on the banks of the Saint Lawrence River and a new civilization grew in the wilderness that Cartier had discovered.

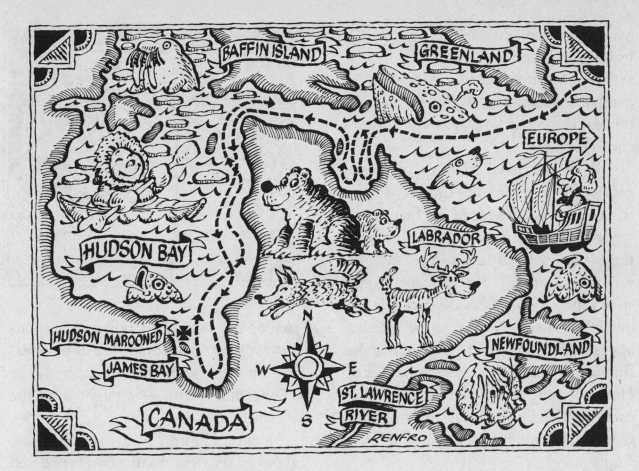

HENRY HUDSON

Henry Hudson was raised in England, but not much is known about his early years. Still, it is safe to say that he must have heard a lot about the great search for the shortcut to the Far East. His father worked for the

Muscovy Company, which was formed by his grandfather and the famous British explorer, Sebastian Cabot. Although the company traded with Russia for furs and timber, its main goal was to find a shortcut to China.

Historians have tried to piece together the early part of Hudson's life. It is believed that he made his first ocean voyage as a teenage cabin boy on one of the Muscovy Company's ships. His job was to run errands for the captain and spend long night hours on deck alert to possible danger. At 16, he became an apprentice and began to learn about the fine art of sailing. After seven years, Henry became a seaman. By 1607 he was such a skilled sailor that the Muscovy Company made him captain of his own ship.

Since the opening of the Age of Discovery, Europeans had explored every important bay, inlet and river along America's eastern coast, looking for a short route to Japan, China and the Spice Islands. Captains from the northern countries of Europe even searched for what was known as the Northeast Passage, around Scandinavia and Russia. But no one had yet found a short route to the riches of the Far East.

Henry Hudson was convinced that a northern shortcut existed and he per-

suaded the Muscovy Company to sponsor a voyage of exploration. His plan was to reach the other side of the world by sailing due north — straight over the North Pole!

Henry Hudson and his crew were about to try what no one had ever dared before. The North Pole was regarded as a land of mystery. Hudson knew that there would be ice and cold, but because he was sailing during the summer he thought that the sunlight would melt most of the ice. Then he would be able to sail through to China. The Muscovy Company hoped he was right.

On April 19, 1607, Captain Hudson and his crew boarded their small ship, the *Hopewell.* Among the crew of 12 was one of Hudson's three sons, John Hudson, who was about to begin his sailing career as a cabin boy. As Hudson steered the ship down the Thames River and into the Atlantic, he began his logbook of the journey. He was a careful observer and planned to write down everything he saw.

For the first month and a half, the weather was good. But as the ship approached the shores of Greenland, the weather changed. Thick fog rolled in and freezing winds tossed the tiny ship about in the heavy seas. Hudson kept sailing north, hugging the eastern coast of Greenland in search of a waterway that would lead them through the island. Unable to find a strait, he turned the *Hopewell* back toward the open sea.

On June 27, the little ship neared a group of islands north of Norway, now known as Spitsbergen. Here the water was calmer and the men saw an amazing sight — hundreds of huge gray whales. Hudson carefully charted the spot and named it "Whales Bay." He knew it was an important find. Whale blubber, used to make soap and fine oils, would bring in great profits.

It was July now, and although it was warm in England, the northern weather was bitterly cold and the sea was filled with ice. As the wind blew, waves crashed over the deck. Suddenly the crew of the *Hopewell* heard a loud boom. A large

fragment had broken away from a giant iceberg and was being blown directly toward the ship. Quickly the crew lowered a rowboat and tried to tow the *Hopewell* out of its path. But their effort was not enough and it looked as if the ice would collide with the ship. Luckily the wind changed course and the *Hopewell* was blown out of the way.

Supplies were now running low. The wind and fog were getting worse and it was clear that there would be more ice farther north. As a result, Hudson decided to turn home for England. He had reached a point just north of 80 degrees latitude and had been 575 miles south of the North Pole, closer than anyone had ever been before.

In the middle of September, the *Hopewell* arrived safely in London. Hudson had been farther north then any other explorer, but he was disappointed that he had not found the shortcut to China. The Muscovy Company, however, was pleased with his discovery of the whales at Spitzbergen.

Henry Hudson was still eager to find a shortcut to the Far East and the Muscovy Company was glad to pay for another voyage. So Hudson spent the winter months studying maps and charts. This time he plotted an eastern route around the North Pole. He knew that he would encounter ice, freezing winds and fog again, so he had the *Hopewell's* hull strengthened with sturdy planks and ordered thicker masts.

Only a few sailors from his previous trip were willing to sail again into the cold north. One was Robert Juet, who signed on as first mate. His son John would be the cabin boy. Hudson's carpenter from the previous voyage, Philip Staffe, also agreed to sail. The rest of the 15 crew members were new.

On Friday, April 22, l608, the *Hopewell* pulled away from Saint Katharine's Docks in London. Once in the Atlantic, the small ship sailed north and rounded the northern tip of Norway. Soon the crew found themselves in an amazing world. It was the Arctic summer, when the sun is visible 24 hours a day. But the air was still bitterly cold and there were towering icebergs moving silently through the sea. It was a beautiful sight, but terrible, too, because the great frozen masses made sailing very dangerous.

In June, the ship found its path blocked by floating ice. Hudson, a skilled sailor, managed to steer through the obstacles. But as the *Hopewell* sailed on, more and more ice appeared ahead. Then it started to pack together behind the ship. Hudson knew that if they did not act quickly they would soon be trapped.

Fortunately he was able to turn the little ship around and steer out of danger.

For many weeks the crew saw nothing but ice. There seemed to be no life at all in these freezing waters. Then in mid-June, a sailor looking over the side saw what appeared to be a strange and beautiful creature swimming in the sea. He thought it was a mermaid. At this time, many people believed that mermaids really existed. The sailor cried out and another sailor joined him. The two men watched the creature in the water until it disappeared. Immediately they reported the sighting to Captain Hudson. In his logbook, the captain wrote: "Her body was like a woman's. She had long hair hanging down behind, of color black, and they say they saw her tail, which was like the tail of a porpoise and speckled like a mackerel." No one was sure what the sailors really saw, but it was an exciting day for the crew of the *Hopewell*.

The crew saw no more "mermaids" after that, only huge amounts of ice everywhere. Hudson realized that it would be impossible to sail any farther north, so he turned the ship toward Novaya Zemlya. The maps Hudson had studied showed this to be a part of the mainland of Asia. He did not know it, but Novaya Zemlya is actually a pair of islands in the Arctic Ocean. Several times, Robert Juet and other crew members went ahead in the rowboat to explore rivers on the coast of one of the islands, hoping to find a passage to China. But each time they were disappointed.

By now the crew was tired of ice, cold and fog and wanted to turn back. Hudson wanted to continue his search, but he could tell that the sailors were on the verge of mutiny. Finally he gave in and turned the *Hopewell* southward toward home.

Hudson docked in England in the fall of 1608. This time the Muscovy Company was not pleased with his report — he had not found the shorter route to China or anything else of value. Although Hudson was also disappointed, he was not ready to give up. He still believed that a short route existed.

In spite of the Muscovy Company's reaction, Hudson was treated as a hero elsewhere. Word of his bold voyages had spread to other countries. The Dutch East India Company invited him to come to Amsterdam. The company's directors were sending out ships to trade in the Far East by the long southern route down the South American coast and across the Magellan Strait. They were eager to find a shorter one. And Henry Hudson seemed to be the right man for the job.

Hudson told the Dutch that he would not return until he had found the passage. The merchants instructed Hudson to search for the passage to the east of the North Pole and not to try any other routes. If he could not find an eastern passage, he was to return home.

Henry Hudson, however, had other plans. He had received a letter from an old friend, Captain John Smith, who was in charge of the English colony at Jamestown, Virginia. The letter said that the local Indians knew of a body of water north of Virginia that led to the Pacific Ocean. Hudson kept the letter a secret, knowing that someday it might come in handy.

The Dutch East India Company gave Hudson a small ship slightly less than 60 feet long, called the *Half Moon*. Although Hudson wanted an English crew,

JAMESTOWN, VIRGINIA — THE FIRST ENGLISH SETTLEMENT

On April 26, 1607, three ships commanded by Captain Christopher Newport and carrying 105 adventurers landed in America. Their purpose was to search for treasure and to spread Christianity among the Indians. The ships sailed up the James River at the mouth of the Chesapeake Bay and landed at a little peninsula on May 14. Their settlement was established near what is now Williamsburg, Virginia. Both the river and the settlement were named in honor of King James I of England.

The Jamestown settlement was a disaster at first. The water was not safe to drink and the adventurers were not willing to do manual labor or to plant crops. Many died of starvation and disease. In 1608, Captain John Smith took control and forced the settlers to stop searching for gold and silver and to start working for their survival. He avoided immediate starvation by buying corn from the Indians and managed to save Jamestown from destruction. In 1610, Governor Thomas West arrived with more settlers and supplies. Over the next few years, the settlement grew and began to supply tobacco, corn and hogs to the European market.

In 1619, when the population was about 1,000, a Dutch ship arrived with 20 blacks for sale. These Africans, as well as the thousands who followed them, became slaves. Their labor helped to make the settlement prosperous. However, in the late 1600s, Jamestown was destroyed by fire. In 1699, the people of Virginia transferred their capital to nearby Williamsburg.

his backers insisted that at least half the crew be Dutch.

Again Hudson hired old Robert Juet and his son John, who was now to sail as an apprentice. With a ship, supplies, an 18-member crew and Captain John Smith's letter, Hudson was ready to sail once more into the unknown.

On April 6, 1609, the *Half Moon* left Amsterdam and headed north. Within a month, Hudson had reached the Arctic Ocean. The Englishmen were familiar with the freezing winds, ice and fog in that part of the world. But the Dutch sailors were used to voyages in the warm southern seas. They grumbled about the ice and freezing cold weather and picked fights with the Englishmen. By the middle of May, the Dutch sailors had rebelled openly and refused to sail any farther north. Faced with mutiny, Hudson knew he had to act quickly. He was not ready to head back to Amsterdam.

To buy time, he brought all the men together and showed them Captain Smith's letter. Hudson told them that this was their chance to find the Northwest Passage. He promised the sailors

at what is now called Penobscot Bay in Maine. Hudson sent men ashore to cut down a tall tree for a new mast and to refill the ship's water casks. The sailors also caught enough lobsters to fill many baskets.

The Indians were friendly. But for some reason Robert Juet believed they were planning to attack the ship while the crew was asleep. To head them off, he led a raid on the Penobscot village. The Indians fled when Juet and his men fired their guns. Then the sailors stole whatever they could and returned to the ship.

Hudson was angry at Juet for stirring up trouble. He believed that the Indians had never meant to do them any harm. But now they would probably seek revenge. So he ordered the crew to raise the anchor and headed the *Half Moon* south.

By the middle of August, the ship had reached the coast of Virginia, near the Jamestown Colony. Wild storms prevented a landing and Hudson, eager to search for the Northwest Passage, did not visit his friend Captain John Smith.

Hudson turned the *Half Moon* around and sailed north, hugging the coastline and exploring every nook and cranny. He sailed briefly into the Chesapeake Bay and up the Delaware River, but neither proved to be the passage west.

Then the small ship headed north

that they would be richly rewarded. To his relief, they agreed to change course. The *Half Moon* turned around and headed west.

On June 5, the lookout in the crow's nest sighted the coast of North America through the mist. The *Half Moon* anchored in a large bay for several days, waiting for the weather to clear. Then, out of the mists, there appeared two canoes filled with Penobscot Indians. They were used to trading with French fishermen and came aboard. But the sailors had never seen Indians before and were afraid. Eager to make friends, Hudson gave them trinkets that he had brought to trade for spices in China.

When the fog lifted, the sailors saw that they were in a beautiful bay, with thick, green forest all around. They were

IN SEARCH OF THE NORTHWEST PASSAGE

Many men tried to find the Northwest Passage to Asia. Some explorers made important discoveries in the attempt. Others died trying. Although the French failed, they made important discoveries in Canada.

England searched as well. Sir Martin Frobisher sailed past Greenland and on to Baffin Bay in 1576. After Henry Hudson's discovery of Hudson Bay in 1610, another explorer, William Baffin, who discovered the bay that bears his name, found a waterway between two Arctic islands. This is now called Lancaster Sound. Baffin was unable to sail through it because of thick ice. If he had been able to continue, he would have discovered the Northwest Passage.

It was not until 1903 that the first successful voyage was made through the passage at the top of the world. The man to make the trip from the Atlantic to the Pacific Ocean was a Norwegian explorer named Roald Amundsen.

It is ironic that after so many people went to so much trouble to find it, the Northwest Passage is not used much today because of ice and storms.

---

along the sandy coast of what is now New Jersey. On September 3, 1609, the *Half Moon* rounded Sandy Hook and Hudson found himself at the mouth of a vast open bay — the Lower Bay of New York harbor. In the distance, a waterway led inland. Judging from the strength of the current flowing out of the bay, Hudson believed that it had to be the mouth of some great river or strait. He reasoned this was the passage that Captain Smith had heard about from the Indians.

Hudson steered the *Half Moon* into the bay. Although he did not know it, this was the same bay that Verrazano had entered 85 years earlier. The ship sailed past what is now Staten Island, Coney Island in Brooklyn, and the tip of Manhattan Island into the Upper Bay and the river beyond. Hudson did not know if the water was deep enough for the *Half Moon*, so he sent a rowboat ahead to check the depth. The sailors used a long line with a lead weight attached to measure the depth of the water. As they dropped the line again and again in front of the ship, they reported safe depths.

There were many Indians in the region and they paddled out to the *Half Moon* to trade tobacco for knives and beads. Dressed in feathers, furs and skins, the natives had copper tobacco pipes and the women wore copper necklaces. Some of the *Half Moon*'s sailors went ashore and brought back dried currents, which they had never tasted before. Juet, who

peared to lead to an open sea. Excitedly, they turned back to report what they saw. By this time, the sun had set. Suddenly two canoes sped out of the darkness toward them. Before the sailors knew what was happening, arrows flew toward them. They were forced to row for their lives and load their guns at the same time. Then it started to rain, which drenched their gunpowder. One sailor was killed and two others were badly wounded by the arrows. The other two men kept rowing in the darkness until they no longer heard their pursuers behind them. In the morning, the *Half Moon* found the rowboat with the five men aboard.

After this run-in with the Indians, some of the crew wanted to turn back. But Hudson continued to sail up the broad, magnificent river. The fever to explore was burning in him. His logbook also shows that he was greatly affected by the natural beauty of the surrounding countryside. It was autumn and the large trees were scarlet and gold. In the distance he could see the mountains that would eventually be known as the Catskills. Hudson called the waterway, "The Great River of the Mountains."

Indians came out of the forests to see the strange ship as it sailed by. The crew was on guard, ready for any trouble. Yet Hudson saw fit to allow some natives to

kept the ship's log, reported that the fruits the Indians gave them were "sweet and good." But he also made another notation about the Indians: "We dare not trust them."

In the weeks that followed, the *Half Moon* sailed up the river and encountered many different Indian tribes. Some were peaceful and friendly. But other tribes were more warlike. On one occasion, five sailors were rowing well ahead of the ship to measure the depth of the water. They reached a place in the river where it ap-

A PROBLEM WITH THE COMPASS

Icebergs were not the only difficulty Henry Hudson had to contend with while sailing in the Arctic Seas. A big one was the compass. This all-important instrument was based on the discovery that a magnetized sliver of iron will always point toward magnetic north.

The first compass was used in the 12th century. It consisted of magnetized iron attached to a wood splinter floating in a bowl of water. By the 16th century, a magnetized needle was suspended on a pin above a card marked with the four directions — east, west, north and south. The card was enclosed in a bowl that was held in place by swivels so that the compass would remain level on a tossing ship.

Explorers eventually discovered that there is a variation between magnetic north and true north, something that even Columbus noticed. For Hudson, this problem was more severe, since the compass variation increases as one goes farther north. As a ship sails closer to the pole, the difference between magnetic and true north becomes greater and greater, until finally the compass becomes useless. Today satellite navigation helps to solve the problem.

come aboard; and he and other crewmen even went ashore for a visit. They had dinner with the Indians and returned after a short time to the ship. Hudson recorded in his log, "The natives are a very good people." He added, "When they saw that I would not remain, they thought I was afraid of their bows. Taking the arrows, they broke them in pieces and threw them into the fire."

When the Indians visited the ship again, Hudson gave them wine in return for their kindness. The Indians had never tasted alcohol before, and it made them feel quite merry.

Hudson did not want to lose any more time and continued to sail up the river. The *Half Moon* sailed about 150 miles up to where Albany, New York, is today. The river, which had till this point been wide and deep, now became narrow and shallow. The ship began to sail up what is now the Mohawk River, but the water became too shallow for the *Half Moon*. Hudson realized that he had reached a dead end. This was not the Northwest Passage and once again he would have to turn back.

Disappointed, Hudson sailed back down the river toward the Atlantic. On the way, many Indians came aboard the *Half Moon* to trade. For the most part, they were friendly. Then one day trouble began. Robert Juet, who did not trust the

Indians. The natives had never seen such powerful weapons before and fled into the forests. But after a while, they gathered their courage and attacked again, following the *Half Moon* downriver. Four more Indians were killed when Juet blasted their canoe to bits with the falcon.

The *Half Moon*, faster than the canoes, finally left its pursuers behind and soon sailed out into the Atlantic Ocean. Hudson wanted to continue looking for the Northwest Passage, but the crew wanted to go back to Amsterdam. They were uncontrollable at this point and Hudson saw that there would be trouble if he continued the voyage. So he headed the *Half Moon* east across the Atlantic.

On the way back to Amsterdam, Hudson docked in England on November 7, 1609. He and his son John went to London. From there Hudson sent a letter to the Dutch East India Company, proposing another voyage to the north. When the Dutch read the letter, they were angry and would not even consider another voyage until Hudson returned to Amsterdam with the *Half Moon* and a full report on his explorations.

On their part, the English were angry with Hudson because he had claimed his discoveries for the Dutch. They wanted to keep the New World under British control. Before Hudson could answer the

natives at all, caught an Indian stealing some things from his cabin. He shot and killed the man on the spot. The rest of the natives on board jumped off the ship at the loud sound of the gun. The sailors, still angry about the murder of one of their crew members, went after the fleeing Indians in the rowboat. But Hudson ordered the men back because he expected much more trouble if the ship remained in the area. He raised anchor and set sail as quickly as possible.

Twenty miles downriver, the *Half Moon* rounded a bend to find over 100 Indians armed with bows waiting on both shores. As the white men sailed by, the Indians loosed a barrage of arrows. Canoes tried to get closer to the ship, but Hudson's men fired back. Using a small cannon called a falcon, Juet killed several

IN SEARCH OF THE NORTHEAST PASSAGE

Jealous of the rich Portuguese and Spanish merchants who traded in Asia, the English began to sponsor expeditions to find a Northeast Passage in the late 16th century. The first expedition was led by Sir Hugh Willoughby and Richard Chancellor in 1553. A storm off Norway forced their ships ashore, where Willoughby died. Chancellor, however, went on and reached the mouth of the Dvina River in northern Russia. There he met representatives of Czar Ivan (the Terrible). His voyage led to the founding of the Muscovy Company and trade with Russia.

In the 1590s, the Dutch entered the search for the Northeast Passage. Willem Barents made three voyages into the Arctic Ocean, and in 1596 he discovered Spitzbergen, now part of Norway. Barents died on his return voyage.

In 1728, a Danish explorer named Vitus Bering, who had originally been employed by Russian emperor Peter the Great to explore the Pacific coast of Russia, discovered the strait that separates Russia from Alaska. The strait also joins the Pacific Ocean and the Arctic Ocean. It now bears his name.

The first successful voyage through the Northeast Passage was made during 1878-80 by Nils Nordenskiöld, a Swedish explorer. The route is now an important one for Russian ships, although vessels known as ice breakers must be used to navigate the icy waters.

---

letter from the Dutch merchants, the British government ordered Hudson to make future voyages in the name of England. Hudson agreed.

Although Dutch members of Hudson's crew did eventually sail the *Half Moon* back to Amsterdam, the Dutch East India Company never did get Hudson's journals and charts. The Dutch were quite angry, but there was little they could do.

Hudson still believed that he could find a westward water route to China. The English believed one existed, too. And if anyone could find it, they thought Henry Hudson could. A wealthy group of Englishmen put up the money for his next voyage and provided a small ship named the *Discovery*. This time Hudson was allowed to choose his own crew. He hired his son John again, as well as his loyal carpenter, Philip Staffe. Hudson had his doubts about Robert Juet because the man had stirred up so much trouble on the last voyage. But he was an experienced mariner, especially in the New World. So Hudson signed him on again.

On April 17, 1610, the *Discovery* set sail from London. From the very start, there was trouble. Five days into the voyage, Hudson fired his assistant, a man named Coleburne, who had been hired by the merchants. The *Discovery* then docked at Gravesend, England, where Hudson hired a young man named Henry Greene as his new assistant. He already knew Greene and liked him, but he overlooked the fact that the man had a violent temper and was known as a troublemaker.

The *Discovery* left England and headed northwest, reaching Iceland in 11 days. But fog and bad weather forced Hudson to sit at anchor for two weeks, waiting for the weather to clear. Young Henry Greene became restless and, for no reason at all, he started a fight with the ship's doctor. Hudson, who seemed to favor Greene, did not blame him for the fight. This made Juet angry at the captain, and he began to stir up the crew against Hudson.

On top of that, nature seemed to conspire against Hudson. In those days, many sailors believed that evil spirits lived inside volcanoes. It was Hudson's luck that just as the *Discovery* sailed past Iceland's volcanic Mount Hekla, fiery, molten rock shot out from its mouth. The crew members believed that the erupting volcano was a sign of bad weather. By coincidence their superstition seemed to hold true. As the *Discovery* tried to leave, it was blocked by ice. When Hudson tried again, the winds blew the wrong way. It was June 1 before

he could finally sail clear of Iceland.

On June 4, Hudson rounded the southern tip of Greenland and sailed westward through ice-clogged seas to the mouth of what is now called Hudson Strait. The entrance to this strait was discovered in 1585 by the English explorer John Davis, who called it the Furious Overfall. He never entered it because the water swirled, bubbled and foamed furiously. The *Discovery* almost became trapped in the treacherous waters, but Hudson was able to pilot the small ship safely through — only to be met by gigantic icebergs.

Hudson slowly guided the ship among the huge blocks of ice. But gradually the ice became thicker. As Hudson tacked north and south to find openings in the ice, the sailors became terrified.

Soon another rebellion was brewing.

Hudson was also worried that their little ship would be crushed by the ice, but he was not going to give up. He convinced the crew that if they went a little farther, the weather would begin to turn warm again. Little by little, the *Discovery* inched forward through the ice.

On August 3, 1610, Hudson saw the strait widen into a great sea that stretched further than he could see. At last he had reached the northwest sea route to the Pacific Ocean. Or so he thought. This huge body of water is now known as Hudson Bay. It is an inland sea in one of the coldest regions of world, where the water is frozen solid for more than nine months of the year.

Hudson sailed south along the eastern shore of the enormous bay. He found a place to anchor and named it the Isles of God's Mercy. The first thing he did was send men ashore to hunt for food. But the land was barren and rocky and the sailors could find none.

For the next few weeks, the *Discovery* sailed along the coastline through ice and fog, searching for a safe place to anchor. When Hudson found one, he again sent a group of men ashore. The land here was covered with grass and the sailors wandered about in search of anything that could be eaten. It seemed that the area was totally without life. But then the sailors came across a very strange sight — mounds of stones, shaped like huts. When they lifted the top stone off one of the mounds, inside was a long row of birds hung on a stick. Food! It turned out that Eskimos had built the mounds to store their game for the winter.

The sailors began to load the birds into the rowboat, when they heard the sound of a shot from the *Discovery,* signaling them to return to the ship. Back on board, they showed Hudson what they had found. They were eager to load the ship with all the birds inside the mounds. But Hudson refused because he was in a hurry to get through what he thought was the Northwest Passage before winter set in. The days were already getting colder and shorter. He promised the men that they would reach the Far East by February if they kept going. So the *Discovery* sailed on.

Early in September, the little vessel sailed into what would eventually be known as James Bay. Old Robert Juet, the first mate, began to criticize Hudson's decision to continue the voyage. He told the crew that the captain's promise to reach the Far East by February was a big joke. He urged them to keep their weapons ready for a mutiny. But Hudson found out about Juet's plans and replaced him with a man named Robert Billet.

A short time later, an ice storm prevented the *Discovery* from sailing. After eight days, Hudson could wait no longer. He ordered the crew to raise the anchor and head out into the storm. Hudson pushed the *Discovery* at a furious pace, even sailing in the dark, in spite of the ice and shallow water. One night the ship grounded on some rocks and the crew had to work 12 hours in the bitter cold to free it. Hudson tacked east, west, north and south, maneuvering through the ice. He became obsessed with his search for a passage to the Far East. It seemed that his men no longer mattered to him. In fact, they were only in his way.

Hudson even went so far as to gather up all the sailors' journals so they could not keep track of their location. Then he fired Billet and replaced him with John King, who was unable to read or write or figure out Hudson's charts. Now only the captain would know where the *Discovery* was heading.

By the end of October, winter had set in and Hudson finally had to admit that they would be stuck in this frozen world until spring. On November 1, the *Discovery* was hauled into shallow water at the end of what is now James Bay in northern Ontario, Canada. By the 10th she was frozen in for the winter.

Tension mounted steadily as the long, bitterly cold months passed. Supplies ran low and Hudson put everyone on limited rations. The men were angry and thought that he was hoarding the food for himself. Soon they began to steal food from each other. Everyone was cold, hungry and frightened. Many became sick. When one sailor died, the crew fought over his belongings. Juet and Greene fought constantly. Hudson now thought that Greene had become disloyal and yelled at him in front of the crew.

One day an Eskimo came to the ship. Hudson gave him a knife and some buttons, hoping to trade for some food. The native could not understand English, so Hudson used sign language. The man replied in sign language, saying that he would return after one night. He did return the next day with a sled full of deer skins. But no food! Hudson gave the Eskimo more trinkets and the native made the same signs, indicating that he would come back. Hudson waited and waited, but the Eskimo never returned.

In the middle of June, the ice had broken up and the *Discovery* could leave. Determined to return to England, the crew threatened to mutiny. Hudson must have finally recognized that they were serious because he agreed to turn

FIRST TO THE NORTH POLE

The search for the North Pole is more accurately described as a "race" to see who could be the first to reach it. An American naval officer named Robert Peary won when he and his dogsleds reached the pole on April 6, 1909. The first men to fly over it were Richard Byrd and Floyd Bennett in 1926.

back. Then the crew made him sign a statement that he was returning of his own free will. They did not want to be accused of mutiny when they got home. The penalty for such a crime was death by hanging.

Even though Hudson had agreed to head back to England, he did not order the *Discovery* to sail. He just could not bring himself to give up once again. The crew waited day after day for the order to raise the anchor, but it never came. Members of the crew now began to think seriously about mutiny.

Finally, on the night of June 21, Henry Greene went to the cabin of his shipmate, Abacuck Prickett, who kept a journal of the voyage. What Prickett recorded about the sailors' actions was critical. But even more important was the fact that he had once worked for the London merchants who funded the voyage. Greene hoped that if Prickett joined

the mutiny, the merchants would not punish the mutineers too severely.

The plan was to seize the *Discovery* and immediately sail back to England. At first, Pricket would not go along with the plan to seize the ship. He pointed out that they would all be hanged. Greene said that he would rather be hanged in England than starve to death where they were. Pricket finally agreed to help, as long as no one would be hurt.

The next morning, members of the crew took Captain Hudson prisoner as he came out of his cabin. He and his son John, plus John King and six men who were too sick to sail, were forced into the *Discovery's* rowboat. The boat was lowered into the water and towed behind the ship for several hours. Then Greene cut the towline with an axe. The nine men were set adrift on the icy waters of the bay and soon disappeared from sight.

The *Discovery* finally set sail for England. Before the ship left the icy waters, Henry Greene was killed by an Eskimo when he went ashore and tried to steal food. And Robert Juet died of starvation during the voyage. Only eight sailors made it back to England.

Contrary to their expectations, the survivors were not put on trial for mutiny and murder. To the backers of the voyage, it seemed certain that the great northern sea Hudson had discovered was the Northwest Passage to China. The mutinous sailors were the only ones who knew where Hudson had been, and their help would be needed in guiding future explorers.

Five years later, however, all eight sailors stood trial and were found guilty. It is not known what punishment they received.

Hudson and his companions were never heard from again. It is certain that they either froze or starved to death on the bleak, icy waters.

But Henry Hudson was certainly not forgotten by later mapmakers. The inland sea he found is now called Hudson Bay. His name appears all over New York State: the great river he explored is called the Hudson River, and the highway that runs along its eastern bank in Manhattan

is called the Henry Hudson Parkway. There is even a Hudson City in upstate New York and a Hudson County in New Jersey.

Despite the fact that Henry Hudson never found the Northwest Passage, his bold explorations led the way for future expeditions to the North Pole and greatly increased knowledge of the world.

NEW YORK

Hudson's failure to find a passage did not prevent others from exploiting his discoveries. A few years after his voyage up the great river, the Dutch East India Company built forts along its banks in order to trade for fur and lumber. Later, in 1626, a Dutchman named Peter Minuit purchased the island of "Mannahata" from the Indians for the equivalent of twenty-four dollars. Of course, the name later became Manhattan. The Dutch, who claimed this area along the Hudson River, called it New Amsterdam. However, because Hudson was English, England also claimed the land. In the 1600, the English and Dutch fought three wars over the land Hudson had discovered. In 1664, the English gained control of New Amsterdam and changed its name to New York.

CHRONOLOGY

1419 Prince Henry the Navigator of Portugal establishes the first school of navigation in Sagres, Portugal. Portuguese ships begin the exploration of the west coast of Africa.

1420 Prince Henry's captains discover the Madeiras, a group of islands 400 miles off the northwest coast of Africa.

1427 Prince Henry's captains discover the Azores, a group of islands 800 miles west of Portugal.

1434 One of Prince Henry's captains, Gil Eanes, rounds Cape Bojador on the northwest coast of Africa.

1441 Prince Henry orders his captains to kidnap African natives to be sold as slaves in Europe and begins a highly profitable trade for Portugal.

1450 Bartolomeau Dias is born in Portugal. (This date is a best guess by historians.)

1451 Christopher Columbus is born in Genoa, Italy, as Cristoforo Colombo.
John Cabot is born in Genoa, Italy, as Giovanni Caboto. (The place and date are best guesses by historians.)

1453 Moslem Turks capture Constantinople and block the overland trading route from the Indies to Europe. Prices for spices and silks soar.

1474 Portuguese captains pass the equator on the west coast of Africa.

1476 Columbus arrives in Lisbon and works in a map store with his brother, Bartholomeo.

1480 Ferdinand Magellan is born in northern Portugal as Fernão de Magalhães.

1483 Columbus asks King John II of

Portugal to help him finance a voyage across the Atlantic Ocean (known then as the Ocean Sea) to find the Indies. (This date is a best guess by historians.)

1485 Giovanni da Verrazano is born near Florence, Italy. (This date is a best guess by historians.)

1486 Columbus has his first meeting with Queen Isabella and King Ferdinand of Spain in Cordoba. He asks for ships and men to travel west across the Atlantic Ocean to reach the Indies. They tell him to wait until their war with the Moors is finished.

1487 In August, Dias sets sail from Portugal to find the southern tip of Africa.

1488 In January, Dias's ships hit a storm in the Atlantic that drives them south for 13 days.

In February, Dias lands in Mossel Bay on the southern coast of Africa.

On his return to Portugal, Dias discovers the Cape of Good Hope, the southernmost tip of Africa.

1491 Jacques Cartier is born in Saint Malo, France.

1492 In January, Spain wins its war against the Moors in Granada.

In April, Queen Isabella and King Ferdinand finally agree to help Columbus carry out his plans to sail west across the Ocean Sea.

In August, Columbus sets sail with the *Niña*, the *Pinta* and the *Santa María* to what he thinks is the Indies.

In October, Columbus discovers the islands of San Salvador and Cuba.

In December, Columbus discovers the island of Hispaniola (now Haiti and the Dominican Republic).

Columbus's largest ship, the *Santa María*, sinks after being damaged in a storm.

Columbus sets up a colony on Hispaniola named La Navidad.

Ferdinand Magellan serves as a page at the court of the king and queen of Portugal.

1493 In March, Columbus arrives back in Palos, Spain, claiming to have found the outlying islands of China and the Indies. In May, Pope Alexander VI establishes a line running north and south on a map of the Atlantic Ocean that gives all lands and seas west of the line to Spain and everything east of it to Portugal.

In September, Columbus sails

again for the New World, this time with 17 ships and 1,500 men.

In November, Columbus discovers Dominica. Then he lands at La Navidad to find it destroyed.

1494 In May, Columbus sets up the colony of Isabela on Hispaniola and then discovers Jamaica.

1496 In June, Columbus returns to Spain.

1497 In May, John Cabot sets out from England in the *Mathew* to find a shorter western route across the Atlantic Ocean to India.

In July, Vasco da Gama sails from Portugal to round the Cape of Good Hope, and from there proceeds into the Indian Ocean and on to India itself.

In August, Cabot discovers Newfoundland and the North American continent. He sails back to England after having failed to find a passage through the North American continent to the Indies.

1498 In January, Vasco da Gama reaches what is now Mozambique on the east coast of Africa.

In April, da Gama arrives at Mombasa on the east coast of Africa.

In May, Columbus sets out on his third voyage to the New World.

Vasco da Gama lands in Calicut, India, now called Kozhikode. Cabot sets out on his second voyage across the Ocean Sea to explore his earlier discoveries.

In July, Columbus discovers Trinidad.

In August, Columbus discovers Venezuela and the continent of South America. Columbus arrives in Santo Domingo, the new capital of Hispaniola.

1499 In September, da Gama returns to Portugal from India with an agreement to trade directly with India.

1500 In March, Cabral sets out with a fleet of 13 ships on the first Portuguese trading expedition to India. Dias is in charge of four of the ships.

In April, a storm causes Cabral's fleet to get lost and it lands in Brazil on the east coast of South America.

In May, Dias dies when his ship is sunk in a storm while heading toward the Cape of Good Hope from South America.

In October, after his third voyage to the New World, Columbus returns to Spain in chains, accused of mistreating his colonists.

1502 In May, Columbus sets out on his fourth voyage to the New World.

He calls it his "High Voyage."

In June, Columbus discovers Martinique.

1503 In June, Columbus is shipwrecked on Jamaica, where he and his crew remain for a year.

1504 In June, Columbus is rescued from Jamaica.

In November, he returns to Spain.

1505 Magellan is sent on his first sea voyage, joining a large Portuguese fleet sent to the east coast of Africa to drive Arab trading vessels out of the area.

1506 In May, Christopher Columbus dies in Spain.

1511 Magellan captains his own ship as the Portuguese capture the port of Malacca from the Moors.

1512 Magellan sails to the Moluccas (Spice Islands) and then on to the limits of the known world, discovering a number of the Philippine Islands.

1513 Magellan returns to Portugal after eight years in the Far East.

1516 Magellan makes plans to sail to the Spice Islands by sailing west rather than east, hoping to find a waterway (known then as John of Lisbon's Strait) across the South American continent.

1517 Magellan is invited to Spain to lead an expedition to the Spice Islands.

1519 In September, Magellan sets out with five ships from Spain to find John of Lisbon's Strait across South America.

In December, Magellan's fleet lands near what is now Rio de Janeiro in Brazil.

1520 In January, Magellan finds John of Lisbon's Strait, but it turns out to be a wide river, which will become known as the Rio de la Plata.

In March, Magellan's fleet lands at the Port of San Julian on the coast of Argentina.

In April, Magellan's captains attempt to mutiny and are tried and punished. Later that month, the fleet encounters the giant Patagonians.

In October, Magellan discovers a strait passing through the tip of South America, now called the Strait of Magellan. It is too far south to be of much practical use.

In November, Magellan passes through the strait and enters the Great South Sea, which he names Mar Pacifico (Peaceful Sea), now known as the Pacific Ocean.

1521 In March, Magellan discovers the Ladrones Islands (the Marianas) and later reaches the Philippines again. He has now visited the Philippines twice, first by sailing east and then by sailing west. By combining the two voyages, he has become the first man to sail around the world.

In April, Magellan is killed in a battle with natives of Mactan, whom he was trying to convert to Christianity.

In November, Magellan's remaining two ships, *Trinidad* and *Victoria*, reach the Spice Islands.

1522 In September, the *Victoria* drops anchor in Spain with only 18 sailors on board, the few who have survived the historic circumnavigation of the world in a single voyage. In the same month, Verrazano starts to plan a voyage to find a channel north of Magellan's strait that will lead to China and the Spice Islands.

1524 In January, Verrazano sets out from the Madeiras in the *Dauphine* with a crew of 50 to find a strait through the North American continent to China and the Spice Islands.

In March, Verrazano sights the coastline of present-day Wilmington, North Carolina. In the same month, he discovers the Carolina Outer Banks, thinking that Pamlico Sound is the Pacific Ocean.

In April, Verrazano lands in what will become New York Harbor.

In July, Verrazano returns to France after having explored 2,000 miles of North American coastline, without having found a passage through the continent.

1527 In June, Verrazano sets out on his second voyage, intending to sail through the Strait of Magellan. He cannot pass because of contrary winds and heads across the Atlantic to the Cape of Good Hope. Again he cannot pass, so he sails to Brazil and then back to France.

In September, Verrazano arrives back in France.

1528 In April, Verrazano begins his third voyage, this time to find a passage through the South American continent from the Caribbean Sea. He comes within sight of the present-day Panama Canal, which is a man-made waterway through the narrowest part of the continent. In the same month, Verrazano is killed by unfriendly natives.

1534 In April, Jacques Cartier sets sail from Saint Malo, France, to find the Northwest Passage to China.

In July, Cartier discovers the north point of Miscou Island, Chaleur Bay and the mainland of Canada. In the same month, he discovers a strait that will eventually be named after him and sights what is now the Saint Lawrence River.

In September, Cartier lands back in Saint Malo with hopes that the Saint Lawrence River is the famed Northwest Passage.

1535 In May, Cartier's small fleet of three ships set out on another voyage to find the Northwest Passage. In August, Cartier sails up the Saint Lawrence River.

In September, Cartier anchors at Stadacona, an Indian settlement that is now the site of Quebec, Canada.

In October, Cartier sails farther up the Saint Lawrence to an Indian town called Hochelaga, near the site of present-day Montreal.

1536 In July, Cartier returns to Saint Malo with Donnacona, an Indian chieftain kidnapped from Stadacona.

1541 In May, Cartier sets out on his third voyage to the Canadian wilderness. Along the Saint Lawrence River he sets up France's first colony in Canada and names it Charlesbourg-Royal.

1607 In April, Henry Hudson sets sail from England in the little *Hopewell.* His intent is to reach the Far East by traveling across the North Pole.

In June, Hudson discovers Whales Bay off Spitsbergen, Norway.

1609 In September, Hudson, sailing on the *Half Moon,* enters the river that will be named after him in New York Harbor, believing it is the Northwest Passage to China.

In November, Hudson arrives in England without finding the Northwest Passage.

1610 In April, Hudson sets sail in the *Discovery* from London, again seeking the Northwest Passage.

In August, Hudson discovers Hudson Bay, an inland sea in northern Canada.

In June, Hudson's crew mutinies and sets him adrift in a rowboat, along with eight other men. Hudson and his companions are never seen again.

BIBLIOGRAPHY

American Heritage, the Editors of. *Discoverers of the New World.* New York: American Heritage, 1960.

Bakeless, John. *America As Seen by Its Explorers.* Philadelphia: Lippincott, 1950.

Blackwood, Alan. *Ferdinand Magellan.* New York: Franklin Watts, 1985.

Cardini, Franco. *Europe 1492—Portrait of a Continent Five Hundred Years Ago.* New York: Facts On File, 1989.

Clark, William R. *Explorers of the New World.* Garden City: Natural History Press, 1964.

Cottler, Joseph, and Haym Jaffe. *Heroes of Civilization.* Boston: Little Brown, 1931.

—— *More Heroes of Civilization.* Boston: Little Brown, 1969.

Dalgliesh, Alice. *The Columbus Story.* New York: Scribners, 1955.

Delpar, Helen. *The Discoverers: An Encyclopedia of Explorers and Exploration.* New York: McGraw Hill, 1980.

Grant, Neil. *The Discoverers.* New York: Arco, 1979.

Hale, John R., and the Editors of Time-Life Books. *Age of Exploration.* Alexandria: Time-Life, 1966.

Humble, Richard, and the Editors of Time-Life Books. *The Explorers.* Alexandria: Time-Life, 1978.

Lacey, Peter, Editor, Readers Digest. *Great Adventures That Changed Our World.* New York: Readers Digest, 1878.

Levinson, Nancy Smiler. *Christopher Columbus — Voyager to the Unknown.* New York: E.P. Dutton, 1990.

Lomask, Milton. *Great Lives.* New York: Macmillan, 1988.

Lye, Keith. *The Explorers* (The Children's Illustrated Library). Morristown: Silver Burdett, 1990.

Meltzer, Milton. *Columbus and the World Around Him.* New York: Franklin Watts, 1990.

Morison, Samuel E. *The European Discovery of America — The Northern Voyages.* New York: Oxford University Press, 1971.

—— *The European Discovery of America — The Southern Voyages.* New York: Oxford University Press, 1974.

Pennington, Piers. *The Great Explorers.* New York: Facts On File, 1979.

Roberts, Gail. *Atlas of Discovery.* New York: Crown, 1973.

Roop, Peter and Connie, editors. *I, Columbus — My Journal.* New York: Walker & Co., 1990.

Soule, Gardner. *Christopher Columbus on the Green Sea of Darkness.* Lakeville: Grey Castle Press, 1988.

Sperry, Armstrong. *The Voyages of Christopher Columbus.* New York: Random House, 1950.

Sterling, Thomas L. *The Exploration of Africa.* New York: American Heritage, 1963.

Sweetser, Kate Dickinson. *Ten Great Adventurers.* New York: Harper & Row, 1951.

Sykes, Peter. *The History of Exploration.* New York: Harper & Row, 1961.

Syme, Ronald. *Magellan — First Around the World.* New York: William Morrow, 1953.

—— *Cartier — Finder of the St. Lawrence.* New York: William Morrow, 1958.

—— *Vasco da Gama — Sailor Toward the Sunrise.* New York: William Morrow, 1959.

Ventura, Piero. *Christopher Columbus.* New York: Random House, 1978.

White, Anne Terry. *The St. Lawrence Seaway of North America.* Champagne: Garrard, 1961.

Wilcox, Desmond. *Ten Men Who Dared.* Boston: Little Brown, 1977.

Withey, Lynne. *Voyages of Discovery.* New York: William Morrow, 1987.

 INDEX

About The Author

Diane Sansevere-Dreher received her B.A. in Communications from New York University. She has worked in public relations as a marketing consultant in the book, audio and video industries. She is the author of numerous articles published in magazines, including *Billboard, Sight and Sound Marketing* and *Software News*. Ms. Sansevere-Dreher is also the author of three juvenile biographies in the *Changing Our World* series (Bantam Books): *Barbara Bush, Benazir Bhutto,* and *Stephen Biko*. She lives in Pennsylvania with her husband and four children.